My Left Skate

The Extraordinary Story
of Eliezer Sherbatov

Anna Rosner

yellow dog

Copyright © 2022 Anna Rosner
Yellow Dog
(an imprint of Great Plains Publications)
320 Rosedale Ave
Winnipeg, MB R3L 1L8
www.greatplains.mb.ca

Great Plains Publications gratefully acknowledges the financial support
provided for its publishing program by the Government of Canada through
the Canada Book Fund; the Canada Council for the Arts; the Province of
Manitoba through the Book Publishing Tax Credit and the Book Publisher
Marketing Assistance Program; and the Manitoba Arts Council.

Design & Typography by Relish New Brand Experience
Printed in Canada by Friesens

Library and Archives Canada Cataloguing in Publication

Title: My left skate : the extraordinary life of Eliezer Sherbatov / Anna Rosner.
Names: Rosner, Anna, 1972- author.
Identifiers: Canadiana (print) 20220220905 | Canadiana (ebook)
    20220220964 | ISBN 9781773370873 (softcover) | ISBN 9781773370880
    (ebook)
Subjects: LCSH: Sherbatov, Eliezer. | LCSH: Hockey players—Biography. |
    LCSH: Athletes with disabilities—Biography. | LCGFT: Biographies.
Classification: LCC GV848.5.S535 R67 2022 | DDC 796.962092—dc23

ENVIRONMENTAL BENEFITS STATEMENT

Great Plains Publications saved the following
resources by printing the pages of this book on
chlorine free paper made with 100% post-consumer
waste.

TREES	WATER	ENERGY	SOLID WASTE	GREENHOUSE GASES
7	550	3	23	2,990
FULLY GROWN	GALLONS	MILLION BTUs	POUNDS	POUNDS

Environmental impact estimates were made using the Environmental Paper Network
Paper Calculator 4.0. For more information visit www.papercalculator.org

Canadä

FSC
www.fsc.org
MIX
Paper from
responsible sources
FSC® C016245

For Paula
A.R.

For my children, you are my home
E.S.

Contents

Eliezer as captain of the Israeli national hockey team in 2019
ISRAEL HOCKEY FOUNDATION OF NORTH AMERICA
REPRINTED WITH PERMISSION

Chapter 1

Unwanted

MY MOTHER, ANNA, is the strongest person I know. She was a short and solid girl, athletic enough to fight any boy who insulted her. "Call me a name," she would hiss, "and I'll knock out your teeth." As a Jewish child in Moscow, she faced taunts from children and teachers alike. Her religion was stamped onto her school records, so it followed her like a shadow, year after year.

The Soviet Union was a dangerous place for Jews. My mother's grandfather, a proud man, had been imprisoned for ten years for his "Semitic ways," meaning his only crime was practising his religion. My mother's family had the same stubborn pride, though many saw it as foolish. Once a month, they climbed the steps of the local synagogue, staring straight ahead and pretending not to notice the men who watched them from the street. Even as a child my mother knew that government agents wrote the names of Jews in a little notebook to frighten them, or to threaten their families. "Don't look at them, Anna," said her father. "They don't even exist."

There was one place where my mother felt safe and happy, sheltered from the darkness around her: on a skating rink. She received her first pair of figure skates for her fifth birthday, and from then on they never left her feet. That love of ice was something she and I would share our entire lives. She gave up her childhood to train twice a day, both in the early morning and after school. Even though she was the smallest girl on the rink—she never grew past five feet in height, though she longed to—my mother could spin faster and jump higher than any of her competitors. Soon she was winning championships in Moscow and filling her room with trophies.

Years of intensive training in poorly made skates took a toll on my mother's feet. My grandmother would bring her hot water bottles and medicines at night to ease the pain, but nothing helped. No matter how much she hurt, my mother refused to stop training. She just couldn't imagine her life any other way, as though skating were the air in her lungs. When she turned fifteen, her coaches finally offered her a choice: retire from competition or leave home to live and train with other young Soviet athletes who had the same dream.

My grandfather wasn't happy. "You're so young, Anna," he said gently, "and you've had so many injuries. You barely sleep at night. I know you love to skate, but feet can only take so much." As stubborn as she was, my mother knew deep down that he was right. She tucked her skates into a box and didn't touch them again for a decade, too heartbroken to ever return to a rink.

Eliezer's mother and father in the Soviet Union in the 1960s
COURTESY OF THE SHERBATOV FAMILY

When my mother met my father, Alexei, they were still teenagers. He was handsome, with thick, dark hair and olive skin. My parents married young, and my elder brothers, Boris and Yonatan, were born soon after. Though Jews were rarely admitted to universities, my father was a talented student and studied engineering at the University of Moscow. He could fix anything: kettles, radios, and electric heaters. Neighbours lined up at the door with broken appliances, offering him packages of biscuits or whatever money they could find. He always refused to take it.

My father had two great loves in his life: my mother and ice hockey. If there was one thing that brought the Soviet Union together, it was sports. Once a year, everyone in Moscow would gather wherever they could find a television to watch the World Hockey Championships, often broadcast from the West. My father would make pots of hot tea, and he and his friends would crowd into our living room to see the greatest players in the NHL face off against the Soviet Union. The entire apartment building would either groan or cheer in unison after every play. Sometimes people yelled to one another across hallways and down balconies about the referees' bad calls. "Did you see that, Alexei? How is that a penalty? We were robbed!" My father loved it all. He cheered for the Russians but quietly admired Guy Lafleur of the Montreal Canadiens. "Look at him skate, boys," he would laugh. "He's almost flying!" Every Soviet goal sent my father leaping around the apartment and throwing his sons in the air. He was a wrestler and had the strength of a lion.

As my brothers grew older, my parents always seemed to need money to support the family. They counted their savings and found it was enough for my father to start a small company specializing in plastic and bronze. The business became successful in the late 1980s, and the income made their lives easier, for a time. My father was able to surprise my mother for her twenty-fifth birthday by pretending to buy her a pair of tights but stuffing the package with *rubles* instead. She still laughs when she talks about tearing the box and watching the bills and coins fall to the floor.

It wasn't long before trouble found my father; he was Jewish, and he was making a little money. It was a dangerous combination in Moscow. Soon, corrupt officials began to demand payment in exchange for our family's safety. It was money my father couldn't spare, but he paid as many people as he could. Policemen, gangs, even firemen threatened him and stole whatever he had left. He began to look over his shoulder, switching directions on Moscow's streets in case he was being followed. When he arrived home late from work one evening, my mother's face was white.

"What's happened?" he asked. "Where are the boys?"

"They're sleeping, they're fine, *harosho*," she breathed. "Lock the door. Someone was here at the apartment."

My father began to sweat under the heavy coat he was still wearing. "Who was here?"

"A man banged on the door. I couldn't see who it was, you know, because the peephole is too high for me. I stood on the little stool but I didn't recognize him. He kept yelling and pounding on the door with his fists, Alexei! I was so afraid he'd get in. The boys woke up but I told them not to make a sound."

My father collapsed into a chair, exhausted. "Anna," he said, "we can't stay here anymore. They'll never leave us alone. We need to leave Moscow, now. Not in a month, or in a week. Now. Nothing is more important than this family."

My father didn't go to bed. He waited until morning, put on his best shirt, and took the subway to the Israeli embassy, where he stood in a long line with other frightened Jews. He spoke briefly with the people around him, some of them elderly, some of them families with young children, all of them hoping for an easier life in Israel. A long line of sorrows, my father thought. The immigration officer listened to him almost distractedly, as though he had heard the same story a thousand times. "Profession?"

Eliezer's father and grandfather, Alexei and Sergei, pose
in front of images of communist figures Lenin, Marx
and Engels. COURTESY OF THE SHERBATOV FAMILY

he asked. "Number of children? Any family in Israel?" He
worked quickly, staring at the computer screen and typing
everything my father told him. Finally he paused and
looked over his glasses. "You understand the Soviets will
take your citizenship if I issue you Israeli visas?" he asked.

"I understand," said my father quietly. He looked down
at the red and gold passport in his hands. "What difference
does it really make?"

The officer nodded. "It will take some time before the documents are processed," he warned. "Until then, be careful. Be invisible."

For three months, my parents only left the apartment when they needed to, moving through the streets like ghosts. Every day they waited for news of their immigration papers, which finally arrived in the spring of 1989. They gathered my brothers and a few suitcases in their arms and gave all their belongings to my grandmother. They left Moscow, their families, and the lives they knew forever.

∞

IT WASN'T UNTIL 2005 that I first stepped onto a hockey rink in the former Soviet Union, welcomed by cheering fans. My father sat smiling in the stands, snapping photographs for my family and remembering his own father, Sergei, who had loved hockey almost as much as we did, maybe more. I wore the Israeli national team's blue and white jersey, a Star of David decorating my shoulder and chest.

If only, I thought, my grandfather had lived to see this.

Chapter 2

Israel

BOTH MY PARENTS CRIED when they stepped into Ben Gurion airport in Israel. They were free to be Jewish; free to light Shabbat candles, to celebrate Chanukah, and to dream of their children attending university. Still, poverty followed my family to Rehovot, where I was born in October of 1991. Rehovot was filled with Jewish immigrants, some from Russia and Ukraine, others from Ethiopia, all of them trying to rebuild their lives from a few memories. The government gave my parents a cramped two-room apartment they quickly made home. My father arranged their beds beside humming fans and left the windows open to cool the rooms, but he could never manage to sleep through the night. His Russian blood wasn't used to the stifling heat, which soared to forty degrees for weeks at a time.

The Jewish community in Rehovot was good to my parents. Older immigrants tried to help newcomers to Israel, offering them clothes their children had outgrown, toys, and advice on how to survive daily life in the desert. For a

Alexei with his sons Boris and Yonatan in Israel, just before
Eliezer's birth COURTESY OF THE SHERBATOV FAMILY

few months my parents studied Hebrew, becoming friendly
with neighbours and other students in their class. My father
eventually found a job at a telephone company; he spent
his days in the burning sun dismantling unused systems
and lines. Every night he came home exhausted from the
heat. Still, he persevered, convinced that his boys, already
fluent in Hebrew, could succeed in Israel. His family was
safe and that was all that mattered.

In the fall of 1990, my parents received a notice summoning them to the lobby of their apartment building. Israeli soldiers were everywhere, talking and gesturing in different languages, while families rushed back and forth carrying stacks of cardboard boxes and booklets. Frightened, my mother took both my brothers' hands. "What's happening?" she asked. My father shook his head and said nothing.

"Children's masks here!" called an official, waving them over. "How old are your boys?"

My parents realized they were standing in front of boxes filled with gas masks. At first neither one of them spoke. "How old?" he asked again, this time more gently.

"Boris is five," said my mother, "and Yonatan is three." My father's heart fell. For weeks there had been rumours that Israel would be targeted by Iraq, which was at war with the United States and its allies. Iraq's weapons weren't powerful enough to reach the US, but they could strike Israel. Dazed, my father wiped his sweating face and collected four boxes. "We'll never need them, Anna," he promised my mother. He fastened the masks to my brothers' faces to make sure they fit properly, imagining he was somewhere else.

Though no one believed it would happen, on January 17th, Iraq began to launch missiles at Tel Aviv, just thirty kilometres from our home. My parents sealed the apartment with thick layers of tape and kept wet towels by the doors and windows; the bomb shelter was too far away to reach on time. Forty-two missiles fell over a month, always in the night, but none with gas. Every time the sirens wailed, my parents secured my brothers' masks and blocked off the apartment vents. There was nothing to do but sit and wait. Thirty-seven days of war. Now, as a father of two children myself, I can't think about those nights and how my parents must have felt, knowing their children were in danger. The sounds of missiles striking Tel Aviv stayed with them for years.

Healing emotionally was slow for my father, his grief perhaps complicated by some painful news from home received just months before the war: his business partner, who had stayed behind in Moscow, was killed by the Russian mafia. My father was deeply shaken; he had chosen to flee not a moment too soon. "I regret," he said, "living at a time when a human life is worthless." And while my birth after the war was a happy distraction, life in Rehovot was still far from peaceful. Tensions between Israelis and Palestinians weighed on my family. My father's job often brought him to dangerous neighbourhoods and his life was threatened once again, this time by politics he couldn't even begin to understand. Violence seemed to him to be inescapable by then. My parents never truly slept; they wandered to the kitchen in the middle of the night and looked at each other without saying a word, both of them knowing that something had to change. Those months spent in Israel, it was a chapter in their story. It was a new beginning that had saved my father's life, only to endanger it again, or to maybe take the life of one of his sons, who would all have to serve in the army when they turned eighteen. For my father, no stone, no grain of sand in the Middle East was worth the life of any child, Palestinian or Israeli. A year and a half after their arrival, my parents decided to search for a new home, this time in colder temperatures.

My father knew almost nothing about Canada. He did know that it was cold, and that his hockey hero, Guy Lafleur, had played for the Montreal Canadiens. Why not, he thought. As far as he knew Québec was at peace with its neighbours. He filled out pages of immigration forms and sent them to the Canadian embassy. He prepared for his interview by talking to himself in a mirror. "Nice to meet you," he said in his very best English. "I am fine." When my parents were finally summoned, they dressed us in our best clothes, smoothed our blond hair, and boarded a bus to Tel Aviv. On the hour, the driver turned up the radio so passengers could hear the news from Jerusalem.

My mother sat nervously in the lobby of the Canadian embassy while my brothers and I amused ourselves by throwing pens at one other, annoying immigration officers who wandered by. When my father's name was called, he followed an interpreter into a small office with a desk, a Canadian flag, and a few plastic chairs. "Welcome, welcome. Have a seat." The immigration officer held out a hand and addressed him through the Russian interpreter. My father smiled and sat stiffly, grateful for the air conditioning. The officer reached for his papers. "Nice to meet you," my father said, though he realized the officer was Québécois and spoke French.

"So, Mr. Sherbatov," he began. "Can you explain why you want to immigrate to Québec? Why choose Montreal, and not Toronto, for example?" He typed a few words on his computer and leaned back in his chair.

My father glanced at the interpreter, an older woman with glasses and a gentle face. "Should I tell the truth?" he asked her. "Of course," she replied in Russian, "tell him the truth." It was an easy question for my father. He turned back to the officer. "I chose Québec because I want one of my boys to skate like Guy Lafleur of the Montreal Canadiens." Amused, the interpreter translated his answer into French.

The officer leaned forward and stared at him in disbelief. "Guy Lafleur? How do you know Guy Lafleur?" He seemed close to tears.

"Who doesn't know Guy Lafleur?" shrugged my father.

The officer looked at him for a minute and then stood and gave him his immigration papers, still unopened. "You've passed, Mr. Sherbatov," he said, shaking his hand. "I wish you and your family the best of luck in Montreal." My father wandered back into the waiting room, unsure of what had happened. My mother assumed he had failed the interview, which had lasted all of three minutes. My brothers and I continued to throw pens at one another and at a few other kids too. "So?" asked my mother. "What did he say?"

My father looked at her. "I think we're Canadians," he smiled.

A few months later, we boarded a plane for Montreal. I had just begun to walk.

Chapter 3

Finding Home

MY FAMILY ARRIVED IN MONTREAL with exactly $425 and three growing boys. Neither of my parents spoke a single word of French or English, and my brothers spoke only Hebrew and Russian. My father managed to rent a small apartment in LaSalle, near downtown Montreal, for four hundred dollars a month. The remaining twenty-five were used to open a bank account. The apartment was mostly empty, though the landlord had left sugar, rice, and pasta in the cupboards, which we all ate until we could afford to buy some milk and cheese. There were also a few tattered chairs, a kitchen table, and two old mattresses that had somehow lost their beds. One mattress was for my brothers and the other for my parents. That left me with a cold floor.

"He can't sleep on our mattress," said my mother. "Alex, you're built like a Russian tank! If you roll over on him, you'll crush him. Look how small he is." Even at thirteen months I still looked like a baby. Buying a crib was out of the question, so my mother left in search of a bed. She came home a few minutes later carrying a cardboard box for cigarettes.

My father threw his arms up in the air. "Anna, you can't be serious. He can't sleep in that!"

My mother looked at the empty Marlboro box. "Why not? I can make it nice. Just wait." She lined the bottom of the box with a soft blanket and dropped me in. I fit perfectly. "*Voilà*," she said. "You see, Alex. He likes it." I slept in that cardboard box for the next six months of my life, until I outgrew it.

My father desperately needed a job. He wandered the streets of LaSalle and knocked on store windows of any kind: bakeries, hardware stores, and local grocers. Since he didn't speak a word of French, he began to make wooden furniture and sold his pieces to the Jewish community. He was always so good with his hands, whether it was with wood or appliances or machines. Eventually he found a steady job in a factory boxing frozen pizzas. He worked from morning until night, sixteen long hours, so I rarely saw him. We were poorer than we had ever been. Often, my parents didn't eat so my brothers and I could. It's hard for me to think about them going hungry for us, but it happened.

Despite our finances, my father felt at home in the frigid Québec winters, and eventually we began to find a rhythm. My brothers were settling into school, forgetting their Hebrew and quickly learning French, while I began kindergarten and was the smallest child in the class. It was something I had to get used to for the rest of my life,

The Sherbatov brothers shortly after their arrival in LaSalle, Québec
COURTESY OF THE SHERBATOV FAMILY

especially on the hockey rink. I spoke only a few words of French which I had learned from my brothers, but I liked school. My classroom was filled with immigrants, some Portuguese, others Italian or Haitian. Somehow the children all managed to communicate perfectly in ten different languages by pointing, yelling, and flapping their arms. The teachers were lost. I spoke French with a heavy Russian accent that confused them. "Eliezer, we don't pronounce our 'R' like that! Say it with me... *roue, rue, rire.*" But for years I still sounded Russian, rolling my Rs like Alex Ovechkin.

Every day my mother packed me a small lunch in a paper bag, usually a few dumplings or a sandwich. I envied my friends' colourful lunchboxes that were filled with wrapped granola bars, chips, and thermoses with juice, most of which I had never even seen before. The most remarkable thing was that none of my schoolmates ever finished those lunches. That was something I couldn't understand; my brothers and I had always eaten everything on our plates, and lots from my parents' plates too. I wandered around the lunchroom, asking in my most polite French, "May I have your cookie? Are you finished with your drink?" Soon my friends began to bring extra treats for me. I ate three lunches every day and was full and happy.

The first time my father found himself with an extra $500, he knew exactly what he wanted to do: he went to a sports store and bought my mother a beautiful pair of figure skates for $350. She had given everything to us, to the family, and he wanted her to have something she loved, something just for her. My father had never seen her skate before in Moscow, and Montreal was filled with boys who skated everywhere, every day, all of them longing to be the next Guy Lafleur. Everyone talked about the Canadiens hockey team in Québec. Every kid went to bed at night thinking of his next game.

Taking a few more of the dollars he'd worked so hard for, my father paid for the family to go to a local rink in LaSalle. My mother floated onto the ice in her new skates. She hadn't skated for more than ten years, but somehow her feet remembered. Adults and children stopped to watch her spin and jump as she used her powerful legs to circle the rink at lightning speed. My father was amazed. My brothers and I were proud; my mother had the gift every Québécois child dreamed of. And she looked happier than she had in years.

My mother began to coach young skaters for free in the hopes of one day finding paid work. Word of her talents travelled far and fast, and soon every child in LaSalle wanted to be in her class. At first she struggled to communicate instructions to her students, gesturing and showing them the steps herself. "*Oui!*" she would cry when they finally understood. She learned as many skating terms as she could to express herself better in French, and eventually she became a certified instructor. Known in Québec for her Soviet technique and fierce, almost merciless discipline, it didn't take long before my mother was approached by professional hockey players for coaching in power skating. They all towered over her tiny frame.

Seeing my mother on the ice sparked something inside of me. I was six years old, and most of the boys in my school had been skating for years, many as soon as they could walk. My father, who wanted all of his sons to be athletes, decided to enroll me in a hockey league with kids my age. He borrowed skates and a helmet and pushed me onto the ice, his eyes filled with hope.

I fell immediately. Little boys skated past me and looked at me curiously while I lay there in a heap. I tried to get up and fell again. My father looked on with despair; apparently I was not my mother's son.

Eliezer's mother training NHL left winger Anthony Duclair
COURTESY OF THE SHERBATOV FAMILY. REPRINTED WITH PERMISSION

"Get up!" he encouraged me. "Use your legs. Find your balance. Just be strong, in here!" he called, pointing to his stomach. I looked up at him from my tangled heap on the ice and started sliding towards the exit on my hands and knees. My father picked me up in one arm and took me home, trying hard to hide his disappointment.

"Anna," he said. "Skating isn't for Eliezer. He's too far behind. We should probably just sign him up for Taekwondo

Boris (on the chairs), Yoni and Eliezer practise martial arts.
COURTESY OF THE SHERBATOV FAMILY

with Boris and Yoni." My brothers had been studying martial arts for years, and both of them were exceptional athletes. Trophies were starting to crowd our tiny apartment.

My mother wasn't convinced. "Give me a few months with him, Alexei," she said. "I'm a power skater, I can teach him. I just need some time."

"I want to do it," I told them, my heart filling. "I want to skate like the other boys."

My father looked skeptical, but he agreed. He was still hoping for a little Guy Lafleur in the family.

And so began my training regime. Every day after school, my mother arrived with my skates and helmet. I changed in the car, eager to get on the rink. She taught me skating drills that had helped propel her off the ice and into the air as a young girl. She showed me how to push sideways with my legs, to take long strides, and how to lean forward to gain speed without losing my balance. I returned to hockey practice a year later and stepped onto the ice.

I was the fastest kid in the class by a mile. I spread my wings and flew by my teammates like a bird. The coaches didn't quite understand how my mother had done it. They didn't understand it, but they loved it.

I was my mother's son after all.

Chapter 4

Playing for Israel

AFTER SECOND GRADE there was no stopping me on the rink. Hockey became my obsession. If I wasn't actually skating, I was daydreaming about skating, or rollerblading with a hockey stick on the street to sharpen my puck handling skills. My greatest disappointment was that practice was only scheduled twice a week. It just wasn't enough ice time for me. I begged my father to enroll me in two hockey clubs, one in LaSalle and one in downtown Montreal, which was against the rules; a child's address determined which hockey club he could belong to. I decided to wear my father down. "Please, Papa. *Please*. No one will find out. Practice is on Tuesdays in Montreal and Thursdays in LaSalle." At first he refused, but eventually he got tired of listening to me whine and filled out the Montreal forms with a phony address.

During the year, playing for two teams worked beautifully. The problem was the final tournament, when all the hockey clubs in my age group met for the first time. I arrived at the rink and found both my teams calling me over to dress in their jerseys, so it didn't take long for the coaches to figure out what we had done. My father was embarrassed and tried to explain. "He just needed more time on the ice to develop his skills. He loves it. Look at him now," he said. "All the kids call him the Russian Rocket!"

Both coaches grumbled and scolded my father, but they finally decided I could play. I just had to choose a team. Since I really lived in LaSalle, I put on the blue LaSalle jersey and apologized to my Montreal teammates. As luck would have it, LaSalle eventually played Montreal for the gold medal, which put me in a really bad spot. I flew by my Montreal friends and scored three times on a goalie who had been my teammate all year. In the end, it was LaSalle that lifted the trophy into the air. I'm not sure my coaches ever forgave me for that one.

Tournament after tournament, the trophies began to pile up. My mother kept them all, banging nails into the living room walls to make room for medals. I almost always won most valuable player, which didn't sit well with everyone. Hockey was serious business in Québec and parents didn't hesitate to make a nasty comment if they felt their child was being treated unfairly. A controversial call by a referee could start an all-out brawl in the stands, with both words and fists flying. When I was thirteen, I won yet another MVP title and skated over to receive the plaque, though I could barely look at it. My eyes were on my teammate, who was crying, furious that he hadn't been chosen. His father felt the same way and he let my parents have it. I didn't hesitate. In fact, I knew what I wanted to do with the trophy before

Eliezer laces his skates with his teammates.
COURTESY OF THE SHERBATOV FAMILY

the coaches even called my name; I skated to my tearful teammate and handed it to him. "This is for you," I told him. "You can keep it." He wiped his eyes and thanked me, angry at himself for being angry with me. My mother gave me that look I always loved to see, telling me she was proud of me without saying a word.

Despite being MVP, my equipment was often second-rate and almost always second-hand. Paying for lessons, skates, and even the gasoline needed to drive us everywhere was hard on my parents. Still, they chose to give their sons everything they had. Year after year, their sacrifices helped my brothers become Canadian champions in Taekwondo and wrestling and guided me towards a professional hockey career. I think my father felt that if our bodies were strong, our minds and hearts would be too. After all he had been through in his life, he wanted nothing more than that.

Knowing how much my parents had given me, I never complained about my wooden hockey sticks, even when my teammates were playing with the latest aluminum or carbon models. Carbon sticks were over three hundred dollars. I had borrowed them on the ice a few times and was amazed at how light and flexible they were, how easy it was to make a hard and accurate shot. My father was quietly eyeing those carbon sticks too. For my tenth birthday, he came home with a brand-new one in his arms. I almost cried; it was as if someone had handed me a treasure chest filled with gold.

I played with that stick a few times and became a real sniper. I wiped it down after every game and transported it carefully, keeping it beside me in the car. Finally, in one heartbreaking moment, the stick got caught in a broken arena board and snapped in two. I was devastated, not for the loss of the stick, but for wasting the money my father had worked so hard for. I couldn't help myself; I started to sob. My father was still at the arena door, so I skated toward him with the broken pieces in my arms. I didn't know how to look at him. I could barely speak, so I got down on my knees in front of him and cried. Seeing me like that must have been terrible for him. He reached down and took my head in his hands, speaking to me in Russian, as he always did, "*Vso harosho, sinochik*...It's all right, son, it's all right." He wiped my face, pulled me to my feet and promised to buy me another carbon stick someday. That's the kind of man he was, and is.

People in LaSalle knew that I was Jewish, but it had never shifted my hockey journey in any way. I was simply the

Russian Rocket, known as one of the best players in Québec for my age. My success on the rink prompted a few newspaper articles about my life and my parents' immigration from Israel. Eventually, that news reached the ears of Jean Perron, the former coach of the Montreal Canadiens, who had helped the team lift the Stanley Cup in 1986. Perron had been invited to coach the Israeli National Hockey team. He knew exactly what he needed to win: me. He contacted my parents and asked if I was an official citizen. I wasn't. How fast could I get citizenship papers, he wanted to know, and would I play for Israel in the Under 18 World Hockey Championships?

My mother balked. "Under eighteen?" she said, in disbelief. "He's thirteen years old! He still doesn't have a single hair on his chin. He's barely five feet tall. They'll crush him!" Hitting wasn't allowed in Québec in my age group, so I had no experience against the boards. My father saw things differently. Since I was so fast, he figured I could skate away from anyone hurtling towards me with a bone-crushing hit.

"Eliezer will be fine," he announced, "and Israel needs him. Besides, it's Division III. Elie will be the fastest kid on the ice."

Perron agreed. "The team will watch out for him," he promised.

∞

THE 2005 WORLD HOCKEY CHAMPIONSHIPS were held in Sofia, Bulgaria. I had no memory of ever being on a plane, so flying was my first adventure. When we arrived in Sofia in the early morning, I was still half-asleep, but my father was wide awake, glued to the window of our taxi. "The former Soviet Union," he mused, eyeing the stray dogs wandering on the roads. "Almost feels like I never left." It had been sixteen years since he'd fled Moscow with his family and nothing more.

Sofia was a pretty town with cobblestone streets, cafés, and sweet desserts we all learned to love. We settled into our hotel room and fell asleep briefly, only to be woken for the first team meeting in the early afternoon. My father and I made our way to the lobby and found the conference room, where I had the shock of my thirteen-year-old life.

The room was swarming with broad-shouldered, hulking Israeli men who had been shaving for years. They loomed over me like giants. Though I was physically strong, I still had a round baby face and looked like I was eleven. I didn't realize quite how short I truly was until I stood next to them. Coach Perron must have sensed my panic and put a reassuring hand on my shoulder. "Boys, this is our secret weapon," he told them. "Trust me." I shook the players' hands while they all tried to close their mouths. Perron picked up a piece of chalk and started drawing, explaining different strategies and set plays. He was all business.

During our first practice we communicated on the ice in four different languages: Hebrew, English, Russian, and French, with endless translations flying around, so there were always five people talking at once. Perron coached the team in English, but switched to Québécois French to bark instructions at me, which made everyone laugh. Other national teams, like Russia or Canada, meet at least four times a year to practice together and find a rhythm. Skating with a team you know well becomes almost as natural as a heartbeat; you feel your linemates around you and know instinctively where they are. Since the Israeli team had very little funding, players could only meet once in the days prior to every World Championship. In Sofia, we had one week before the tournament began and only an hour of ice time per day. I felt relieved that I was one of the better players on the team, despite my age.

Our very first game was the most intimidating experience of my hockey life. We were facing New Zealand, whose players were also a full two heads taller than me. I was terrified. Five minutes before the puck dropped, I went to the Israeli captain, Raviv Bull, and asked to speak to him. I told it to him straight.

"I'm scared," I said quietly, spinning my stick on the concrete floor. "Look at the size of these guys. They'll crush me."

Raviv looked at me through his helmet visor and nodded. "Do you trust me?" he asked.

"Of course," I said.

"Then believe me when I tell you this: I'll protect you. You understand?" He patted my shoulder. "The other players will figure it out and leave you alone."

It was just one conversation, one sentence, but in that moment, I felt as confident as I had always been. I stepped onto the ice and used whatever speed I had to dodge the

Thirteen-year-old Eliezer fends off an opponent at the World Hockey Championships in Sofia. ICE HOCKEY FEDERATION OF ISRAEL REPRINTED WITH PERMISSION.

beasts skating around me. I was like a little mouse, scurrying through someone's living room while they tried to smack me with a broom. I managed to avoid being hit in my first game and even scored a goal, launching it over the goalie's shoulder. Israel beat New Zealand 7-2, an easy win. We headed to the dressing room to celebrate.

Two days later we played our second match against Australia, the best team in the tournament. By the third period, we were losing badly. We needed goals. I started skating toward centre ice and picked up the puck near the blue line, determined to put it in the net. I saw a clear path to the Australian goaltender and put my head down to gather speed. I never made it. An opponent rushed at me with a full-blown open ice hit, so powerful that I flew backwards and crumpled like a wooden puppet. I was stunned; I think the shock was much worse than the physical pain.

It's not hard to find Eliezer in this photo of the 2005 Israeli National Hockey team (seated second from right). ICE HOCKEY FEDERATION OF ISRAEL. REPRINTED WITH PERMISSION

Somehow I got to my feet and pushed my way to the bench, slowly realizing that nothing was broken. It took me a few minutes, but I recovered.

The Israeli captain had made me a promise and he kept it. Raviv targeted the poor Australian who had hit me on every shift, crushing him into the boards once, twice, three times. By the third period, the bewildered defenseman could barely make it back to the bench. We lost to Australia 7-2, but my teammates had sent a clear message to their opponents: if you want to live, don't touch the kid. I had also learned a valuable lesson that stayed with me for the rest of my hockey career: never, ever, put your head down on the ice.

Chapter 5

Broken

I WAS THE YOUNGEST PLAYER to ever step on the ice at the Under 18 World Hockey Championships. Despite my size, I managed four goals and five assists, and with the talents of two brilliant players, Oren Zamir and Michael Horowitz, Israel won the bronze medal. It was our first ever medal in hockey. I remember my parents and brothers being so proud of me. I was proud of myself.

I think the tournament in Sofia made my dream of becoming a professional athlete much more real, not just for my parents, but for me. When we all watched the Montreal Canadiens on television, I imagined myself on the ice with them, announcing the plays and imitating their shots in my own living room. My father truly believed he was raising a little Guy Lafleur. Though it was a long commute, he enrolled me in École des Sources, a special high school for athletes where we could both study and train in our sport. The last period of every day was devoted to ice hockey. There were athletes everywhere, all of us like family. I was happy there.

I often try not to think about what might have been. How different my life might have been if I had seen my accident coming. It was such a small, insignificant moment. A couple of heartbeats long. It's still hard for me to understand how a few seconds on a road, not even on a hockey rink, could change my life forever. Why hadn't I decided to stay home and watch television that evening? Why hadn't I gone to the gym with my brothers instead of going outside?

When I was thirteen, my family bought our first house in Laval, just half an hour from Montreal. My parents had worked day and night for a decade to be able to give us a real home. I rollerbladed everywhere in Laval, weaving my way through the empty streets, throwing a ball in the air and catching it on my stick. I practised trick shots for hours and taught myself to pass the ball through my legs and into the net.

There was always construction in our neighbourhood; new houses were popping up everywhere, leaving a thin cloud of dust on almost everything. One evening, I went outside to rollerblade as usual after dinner. I remember the heat that seemed to hang in the air from the sun. Maybe I was watching the skyline, maybe I was watching the ball and not the road, I don't know, because I slipped on an abandoned pile of rocks. The weight of my fourteen-year-old body collapsed onto my left knee. For a moment I was stunned, but I managed to take off my rollerblades and walk home in socks. I hobbled into the kitchen and called for my mother.

"It doesn't look too bad," she said, examining my knee. She was used to seeing injuries. "I'm sure it will heal in a few days, if you rest it." By nighttime, though, the pain had worsened, searing from my thigh to my foot. I woke up screaming and crying for my parents. My mother arrived in my room with bags full of ice and taped them to my knee. It eased the pain for a few hours, only for it to return again in the early morning. For days I went through the same pattern. My parents could only watch helplessly, whispering to each other when they thought I couldn't hear. My leg wasn't getting any better. I was anxious to get back on the rink, but skating was out of the question. We finally decided to go to the doctor, and from there, to the hospital.

The doctors weren't really sure what to make of my injury at first. There were consultations, MRIs, and referrals to different specialists, one more confusing than the next. I began to lose feeling below my left knee, as if I only had half a leg. Eventually, the doctors identified the cause.

"What's happening," they explained, "is that there's pressure on the nerve in your knee. That nerve provides sensation to the foot, so when it's compressed by fluid, the muscles can't work and the foot flops down. It's called drop foot. But the good news is I think we can relieve that pressure with a simple operation."

I didn't like the sound of that word. "What kind of operation?" I asked. My father looked at me and immediately answered before the doctor. He put a hand on my arm. "Elie, Montreal has some of the best hospitals in the world, and some of the best doctors are right here in front of us. We have to trust them. This procedure, it's nothing at all. You'll get through it."

I nodded my head. I had to get through it. My left foot had begun to drag on the ground as I walked, and it frightened me. But in truth, nothing frightened me more than the thought of never playing hockey again. So while my teammates were training six times a week on the rink, I prepared myself for surgery. I remember watching my surgeon move quietly under the fluorescent lights of the operating room until everything went dark.

I woke up two hours later to see my parents' relieved faces and my doctor right beside them. She smiled and leaned over the bed. "The surgery was successful, Eliezer," she told me. "We drained the fluid and the feeling in your left foot should return. Soon you'll have more control over the muscle. With a little rehabilitation, of course."

My mother was close to tears. "You see?" she cried. "It's over, Elie. You'll be back on skates in a month." I closed my eyes and imagined myself on the ice, too exhausted to respond.

I began intensive physiotherapy to strengthen my weak leg. I used elastic bands, light weights, and trained in my parents' pool with my brothers. When I could finally feel my toes again I headed back to practice with my old teammates, determined to pick up where I had left off. I was overwhelmed with emotion when I laced my skates for the first time in the dressing room. Everything around me felt so familiar; the faint smell of sweat and powdered hot chocolate, the echo of voices in the arena, all of it was home to me. My friends patted my shoulder and wished me well. "You ready, Elie?" they asked. "I've been ready for six months," I sighed.

The coach blew the whistle to start the warmup drills. I had missed that sound. I felt good skating slowly around pylons, working on technique. Then the coach asked us to skate from one end of the rink to the other, practising stops and starts. That was where I fell apart. Every time I put heavy pressure on my left leg to accelerate quickly, I felt myself losing control. I glided to the bench on one foot, knowing my coach's eyes were following me.

"*Ça va*, Elie? Everything ok?" he asked. I knew I would cry if I answered him, so I just shook my head and made my way off the ice, certain that I had reinjured myself on the first day back. One of my teammates followed me into the dressing room. "It'll be all right," he said, watching me pull off my skates. "You just came back a bit too early, that's all." I nodded, lowering my head behind my helmet cage so he couldn't see my face. I left the dressing room silently and sat alone on a bench, waiting for my mother to arrive.

I began to fall more, not on the ice, but outside on the street. The doctors consulted and again were uncertain; they couldn't understand why the procedure had failed. In the months that followed, my leg became thinner and weaker, seeming to almost separate from my body. My father took me to acupuncturists, physiotherapists, and even tried Chinese medicine. Nothing helped. My situation was stunning to me and to everyone else. I woke up every day and imagined that I wasn't living my own life. I wasn't the boy who had fallen over a pile of rocks on a road; that was some other kid. But the truth was that I couldn't even remember Elie Sherbatov.

The doctors, however, were not giving up so easily. A second operation was scheduled eight months after the first to drain the new fluid, and again they declared it a success. I began to recover some strength and feeling in my leg again, and though it never came back completely, I was able to walk without dragging my foot. I returned to the hockey rink a second time with fire in my veins.

This time it was over within a few days; the nerve collapsed almost immediately under the pressure of my skate striking the ice. The MRIs and consultations began again. Even when I was awake, I felt as though I was caught in a slow-turning wheel, wandering though a terrible dream I'd seen and lived a hundred times before. Seven different doctors gathered during a hospital appointment to discuss my injury but offered no other solutions or hope. I lost all sensation below my knee. At night, I cried quietly so no one would hear, knowing that my mother was likely doing the same in the bedroom down the hall.

And then came a different life. One I couldn't even begin to understand. After the second operation failed, I was completely out of place in a high school filled with talented athletes. I wasn't a hockey player; I was a disabled fifteen-year-old kid, broken like an unwanted toy. If I didn't lift my foot high enough using my hip, I would fall face first, sometimes in the halls of my school. I felt humiliated. I left École des Sources. I lost my school, my hockey friends, and the game which I had loved for ten years of my life.

My sadness and shame turned to anger. I lashed out at my family, knowing, inside, that nothing was their fault.

If my parents even looked at me wrong, I attacked them. My brothers did everything possible to encourage me, but it hurt to watch them excel in martial arts, bringing home a new coloured belt every six months. Mostly I just stayed in my bedroom doing nothing at all.

"Elie," called my father, knocking on my door one evening, "I have something to show you." He held out a newspaper with hope in his eyes and tapped on an article. I glanced at it. The headline was about a player who had come back to the NHL two years after a severe injury. "You see?" he said, brushing my hair off my forehead. "It *is* possible. It's all possible. You can't give up on yourself."

I said nothing. I just pushed the article into his hand and turned my back on the person I loved most. He left my room silently, taking the paper with him. I closed my eyes and buried my face in a pillow. I was furious at the world, at my leg, at a pile of rocks. I hated myself for letting my father down, for destroying the hockey dream he had created for me. I hated myself because I believed I had broken his heart.

At my new high school, I tried to begin my new life, or I pretended to. I didn't really know how regular kids behaved because I had never had any free time to myself. While my new surroundings didn't change my physical condition, I was lucky enough to make a friend, Somaly, who eventually became my girlfriend. In many ways, Somaly and I both carried the weight of history on our shoulders; her parents had immigrated to Québec as refugees fleeing devastating violence in Cambodia. Somaly and I talked about our families and the lives they had lived before us, about my injury, school, everything; we understood each other completely. She was the only person I could spend time with without feeling angry. Somaly existed outside the sports world, and she showed me that life could be bigger than hockey, though I still ached to be on the ice. I felt relieved Somaly didn't know the Eliezer from before my accident, whoever he was. For her, I wasn't a hockey player; I was simply a regular boy with a limp.

Eight more long months passed after my second operation. On the rink, my old teammates were beginning to shine as future NHL prospects, and some even started talking about being drafted. At age sixteen, I had completely given up all hope of playing professional hockey; the two-year break meant that I had fallen too far behind to even consider competing with anyone my age. My mother, however, had other ideas.

"Elie," she said, "I know you don't want to talk about this, but I've been training a new athlete at the rink and he happens to have a father who's a very famous doctor. He specializes in knee surgery. I told him about you and he said his father would see you." She looked at me anxiously.

I was furious. I slapped the kitchen table with my hand. "Mum, it's been almost two years! I just can't do this again. It's over. Do you understand? It's *over.*"

My mother tried to reason with me. "Don't you owe it to yourself to try? You've been so unhappy. Just listen to what this doctor has to say! Maybe he can help you regain a little feeling in your leg. What harm can it do?"

I turned my head away; it was so hard to see her holding back her tears. "One more," I told her. "One, and that's it." I agreed to see one last orthopedic surgeon for my parents, who had probably suffered more than I had from my injury.

That consultation was the first time in two years that anybody had offered some hope. "I can stop that leak permanently," the doctor assured us, "and that will take the pressure off the nerve. What I can't know is if any feeling will come back. That we'll have to see, but I doubt it." I was prepped for my third and final operation, which accomplished all that the surgeon had promised. But after two long years of fluid on the nerve, the damage was permanent. No amount of rehabilitation would bring back the sensation below my left knee. My foot would drag behind me for life.

Which, of course, meant that I could never play hockey again in everyone's opinion. Everyone, that is, except my mother.

Chapter 6

Healing

MY MOTHER BELIEVED. She believed in herself, in her ten years of Soviet training as a figure skater, and in her ten years coaching elite Québécois athletes. "You'll skate, Eliezer. You just have to give me everything you have. All your strength, all your courage. And you have to be prepared to fall and to get right back up. To fall again and again." She also believed that my entire body had to be strong enough to compensate for my weak leg. I intensified workouts with my brothers at the gym, gaining weight and muscle every month. I practised Ju-jitsu, Muay Thai, and other martial arts. At five foot six, I became as wide as I was tall.

For the first few weeks on the rink I flopped around like a fish out of water, slipping and sliding and cursing under my breath. My mother wasn't discouraged; she had taught me to skate when I was six years old and she would do it again at sixteen. "Keep trying," she insisted. "Again. Slow down. Bend your knees. Again." She knew my skate was acting as a brace to keep my foot straight; she just had to figure out a way for me to propel myself forward and regain my speed. "Lift from the hip!" she yelled. "Feel your leg above the knee. Your foot is there, you just have to *believe* it's there!"

In a month or two, I was skating. It was messy, but I was skating. My father decided I needed some real incentive to train hard. The leak in my knee had been fixed, which meant I could relearn any skill without injuring myself further. I dreamed of returning to the Triple-A hockey league, the highest level for boys my age. I just needed someone to take a chance on me.

In January of 2008, a few months after my sixteenth birthday, my father called the general manager of team Laval-Bourassa, Bob Plante. Knowing my reputation as a strong skater, Plante agreed to let me attend one practice with the Triple-A players, just to see if I could keep up. Even though I wasn't completely steady yet, I was overjoyed at the idea of trying.

It turned out to be a wobbly skate, but it was enough to pique the coaches' interest. I had my powerful upper body on my side, which meant that I still had a deadly shot. I used every ounce of my strength to fire lightning-fast pucks at the goalie and found the back of the net more than once. I felt good; I opened my wings and I flew. My coaches loved that energy and determination, that joy. Though my leg confused them because they saw I couldn't walk properly, it was pretty clear that I could and would compete again. The question was whether I was strong enough to play at the Triple-A level. I skated over to the coaches after practice and started talking too quickly.

"I know I was a little shaky," I said, pulling off my helmet. "But this is really the beginning. I've only been relearning how to skate for a month or two. Soon I'll be the player I used to be, I promise you that. Coach Wilsey, you know my mother, she's a power skater. She's training me." I had to stop talking to catch my breath.

The coaches looked uncertain. "We hear you, Elie," they said. "You're clearly an athlete, there's no question there. But we're not sure you're at the Triple-A level yet. Let's re-evaluate your skating in a few months, okay? Maybe you can attend training camp in the fall."

That was all the motivation I needed. I had eight months to prepare for the 2008-2009 hockey season. I practised with my mother every day after school, often for hours. She eventually understood that sheer speed would be my weapon for a strong return to hockey. I still needed to slow down to make a turn on the ice, so if I accelerated faster than all my opponents, I had one extra half-second to steady myself by the time they caught up. I learned how to explode down the ice after the puck, using other powerful muscles in my legs and core. I practised hockey drills and puck handling, continuing to improve my dangerous shot; somehow my hands remembered what to do, even if my mind had forgotten. In ten months, my mother erased those two lost years and found the athlete I had always been. All the pain, both physical and mental, began to fade. I was ready.

When Laval-Bourassa's 2008 season began, Coach Wilsey was expecting me at training camp, but I didn't tell any of my teammates I was returning. I just showed up in the dressing room, two and half years after I had left it. "*Allô* everybody!" I smiled. I'll never forget the looks on their faces, or the eruption of noise; the yelling was so loud that a few coaches poked their heads in the room to see what was happening. I hugged everyone I knew, even my fiercest rivals. The teammates I hadn't kept in touch with wanted to know where I had been. Some went quiet when they saw me walk. My disability wasn't really visible on skates, but it was obvious in shoes. I told them all what had happened.

"But how will you play if you can't feel your leg?" they asked.

"I'm still learning," I told them, not really sure of the answer myself. "I guess we'll see what happens tonight."

I laced up my left skate hard and made my way to the ice, already sweating from nerves. I had exactly seven days to convince the coaches that I deserved to win my spot back. The competition in Triple-A training camp was fierce: there were almost a hundred hopeful players and only twenty-five spots. I had no idea how good my teammates would be. Had they surpassed me entirely? Would the two and half seasons away be one month too many? I closed my eyes briefly before I stepped on the rink and thought about my mother's words: *you're not going to glide on the ice, Eliezer. You're going to run.*

Our coach blew the whistle. "Ok boys, we're going to start with some drills." My heart was pounding. I shifted my weight from one skate to the other, reminding myself that my leg was still there. "Let's skate to the blue line," he continued. "Drop down to the knees and then stand up. Skate to the next line and do it again. Knees, back up. Do it ten times. Then bring it back here."

I took off like lightning and found myself first on the blue line. I dropped to my knees slightly slower than the rest, but because I was such an explosive skater, I caught back up immediately. Skate, knees, up, accelerate. I finished the ten rounds faster than anyone on the ice. I was elated. "Elie, are you trying to make everyone look bad on your first day back?" joked the coach. I smiled at him, grateful that he couldn't see how emotional I was behind my helmet cage. A few of my teammates didn't look too happy with me; not everybody wants the competition.

I played some of the best hockey I've ever played in my life that week, scoring at least two goals in every exhibition game. At the end of training camp, Coach Wilsey thanked everyone for trying out and announced that he and Bob Plante would meet each player individually to discuss the final cuts. I stood in a long line with my teammates who were mostly silent, each of us tangled in our own thoughts. Players left the office either overjoyed or in tears. For those who had been cut, we could only pat them on the shoulder; we knew better than to try to console them with words.

When my name was called, I walked into the office and sat nervously in a chair. Coach Wilsey simply held out his hand. "Welcome back, Elie," he smiled. I don't have words to describe how I felt at that moment. After two and a half years, I was a hockey player again. A good one.

Eliezer's current brace attaches around his shoe to keep his left foot from falling. COURTESY OF THE SHERBATOV FAMILY

The 2008-2009 season was one of the best Laval-Bourassa has ever had. We were brilliant on the ice, all of us. Every game taught me something new about how to move, how to slow down, and what not to do with my leg. I probably fell more than usual, but because I was so quick, it never really mattered; I always had time to get up, to turn, to score. That season, I picked up exactly where I left off. I had 29 goals and 32 assists, for a total of 61 points in 45 games. I finished the regular season as one of the Triple-A league's highest scorers in Québec, and third in points overall. Thanks to my mother, I was unstoppable. Sometimes I think my own joy gave me that strength, that belief in myself that helped me rise to the top and reclaim all that I had lost. Every minute on the ice felt like a gift to me.

My dramatic comeback to hockey created quite a stir, and I was interviewed by a few journalists.

Laval-Bourassa headed into the playoffs as the number one team in the league. Our eyes were on the Triple-A trophy, but we needed to defeat Trois-Rivières in a best of seven series to get it. After three definitive wins, we found ourselves in game four, battling for the championship on home ice. We were down 3-2 late in the third period and the clock was ticking. I was a mess of nerves and adrenaline; game fours are always the hardest to win. Suddenly I caught a pass and accelerated toward the goaltender with a defenseman on my tail. As always, he was about a foot taller than me, so I had to find a way around him. I passed the puck to myself as I had practised a thousand times, out of reach of the defenseman, and flipped it up in the air past the goalie and into the net. The Laval crowd exploded; we had the tying goal. All those years rollerblading with a ball had at least counted for something.

We had just a few minutes in regulation time to score or the game would go into sudden-death overtime. Anything can happen in overtime; one small error can turn the tide and cost the better team the game. I was catching my breath on the bench when Coach Wilsey leaned over and shouted in my ear.

"Elie, get out there and get me that goal! Come on boys! It ends here in game four, you understand?" We all nodded. My coach had taken a chance on me, had trusted me, and had never believed my leg would get in the way of a professional career. I owed him this one.

I jumped onto the ice for the change and took off running. If I was going in a straight line, there were very few players who could catch me when I was at full speed. I pick-pocketed a defenseman and looked up at the goalie, who started to back into the net when he saw me rush at him. Always a good sign: it left me some room and gave me wider angles to shoot from. I launched the puck over the goalie's blocker and held my breath. It found its way home. The noise in the arena was deafening. Stunned, I felt the weight of my teammates jump into my arms to celebrate. We were ahead 4-3 with just two minutes left on the clock. I skated back to the cheering bench and yelled to Coach Wilsey, "I've done my job!" He thumped on my back and put his best defensive line on the ice to protect our net. It was the longest two minutes of our lives; no one on the bench could even sit down. Trois-Rivières pulled their goalie for the extra attacker, but we hung on for the win. When the clock hit zero I looked up into the stands at my parents, my brothers, and Somaly, who were all hugging and crying.

I think all of Laval celebrated with us that night. Our win meant that Laval-Bourassa would represent Québec at the Telus Cup, a national tournament where the best team from every province in Canada would compete for gold. That night was so much more than a hockey game for me. It was so much more than a game-winning goal. It was my own private victory over a pile of rocks.

Chapter 7

Shifting

OUR PERFORMANCE AT THE TELUS CUP in Manitoba was a mix of wins, losses, and ties. The less-than-perfect playing was good enough to earn us the bronze medal against the host team, the Winnipeg Thrashers. It was yet another triumph for Laval-Bourassa. Still, I found myself at the end of a season, unsure what the future held. Some of my eighteen-year-old teammates had been drafted into the NHL, but I had been out of hockey completely when the scouts were really watching. Those two and half years were creeping into my mind, and into my future. I had no idea if my performance with Laval-Bourassa would be enough to attract the eyes of the best league in North America.

There was also the usual very big, or very small, problem: I was short. Really short. I was and will always be five foot seven, if I give a good stretch. And although I didn't want to admit it at the time, my disability was surely on every team manager's mind. I knew there had been NHL players who were blind in one eye or hearing impaired, and

Québec's treasure, Maurice Richard, had a misshapen foot due to his many injuries, but I didn't know of anyone who needed a brace to walk like I did, even though I refused to wear one out of embarrassment. I had to face the truth: I did have some physical limitations on the ice. I compensated for them well at my level, but there were some things I just couldn't do. I buried my disability deep in my mind and never really spoke of it unless I was asked. To survive in the world of professional hockey, I needed it to be invisible. I needed to pretend it didn't exist.

I started the 2009 season with Montreal in the Québec Junior League, a top provincial team. I still had hopes for the NHL draft and was determined to prove myself worthy. In my first sixteen games I racked up fourteen points, and it looked as though I would repeat my performance in Triple-A hockey. My coaches were happy, and I felt one step closer to the Canadiens' blue and red jersey. That brilliant beginning, however, came to a swift end.

What was surprising about my hockey career was that I had never been seriously injured during a game, even the most competitive ones. It was rollerblading that had taken so much from me. On the rink, I'd only suffered minor cuts and bruises. Until my first season as a junior, I had felt oddly protected on the ice. Skating was the only place where my disability wasn't visible, where it wasn't a part of me. I felt less vulnerable with a pack of defensemen chasing me than I did walking in the halls of my high school. I actually loved the danger of hockey. I felt like a warrior, there to fight, but to protect my team as well.

All that confidence vanished in one particularly heated game, when tempers flared and the penalty box was filling up. I took a brutal hit on the ice and struck the boards hard. I don't think I even understood what was happening for a few minutes, or why my arm was suddenly immobile. I just sat on the rink in shock, watching as the scene around me became a blur of confusion; some teammates gathered near me, while others retaliated by pushing and shoving. The coaches took one look at me and immediately knew what was wrong: I had separated my shoulder.

I missed a month and a half of games and was only allowed to return to the ice if I wore a shoulder brace at all times. From the outside, I imagine things looked fine, because I did manage a respectable thirty points by the end of the season. Inside, though, I felt different on the rink, a feeling I hadn't experienced before. For the first time in my life I was nervous, cautious even. Caution is dangerous in a hockey game. You have to be sure of yourself and willing to take every risk, especially in the corners. My fierceness, my overconfidence that had come from twelve years on the ice without a scratch, had somehow faded. I was struggling, and it had more to do with my head than my leg.

It didn't help that in April of 2010, I went to Estonia as part of the Israeli national team to compete in the World Hockey Championships, and things didn't go quite as we'd hoped. In one mortifying game, Romania actually beat us 20-0. Israel finished dead last. It just wasn't our year. "Next time," we all promised one another. Win or lose, I knew I would play for Israel for as long as they would let me.

I continued as a Montreal Junior for another season, all of it unsteady. As the months passed it became more and more certain I wouldn't be drafted by the NHL. My confidence was drowning by then, and it showed on the rink. I sat down with my family to think it through.

"Elie, if it's not going to happen here, it can happen somewhere else," said my father. "There's no reason you can't head to Europe to prove yourself and then come back here. You've given yourself a dream to follow, so do it. Do what you love."

I looked down at the table. A contract from Neuilly-sur-Marne, a suburb of Paris, stared back at me. If I accepted the offer, it would be the first time I had ever been paid to play hockey, a step into the professional world. "If I go," I told him, "I'm worried I'll be off the North American radar."

My father shook his head. "If you get your confidence back in Europe, North America will find you, Elie," he promised. "Go and be the player you know you can be. Besides, France is a stepping stone to the Kontinental Hockey League. Start in Paris and make your way to the KHL. They've never had an Israeli player before. You'll be making history."

The KHL was the best league in Europe and Asia combined; lots of NHL players either started or ended their careers there. I picked up a pen and signed the contract, nineteen years young. A month later I boarded a plane carrying everything that mattered to me: piles of hockey equipment, a photo of my family and of Somaly, and a gold Star of David that had belonged to my grandfather, for luck.

Though I didn't know it at the time, 2010 would become the last hockey season I ever played in Canada.

∞

I FELL IN LOVE WITH PARIS during the taxi ride from the airport. It was all beautiful to me: the narrow streets and shop windows, the markets, even the way clouds settled over the river Seine in the morning. For the first month, I stayed in an apartment with a wonderful billet family while I waited for my Russian passport to arrive. Like other Jews who had fled during the Soviet era, Russia returned my family's citizenship to us, offering my father a formal apology more than a decade after his immigration to Israel. When I was finally cleared to play, I packed up my hockey bags and headed to a Paris suburb only twenty minutes away, Neuilly-sur-Marne. Foreign hockey players lived and practised in an area called the 93.

Neuilly was a different world. It was nothing like the Paris I had come to know. There seemed to be no end to the concrete high-rise buildings, most of them with broken windows and doors landlords never bothered to fix. The streets were covered with graffiti. Neuilly was filled with refugees and immigrants who had fled their homes and were trying to make new lives for themselves in France. Most of them were failing, caught between two worlds. Though I knew there was a lot of crime and was warned against certain areas, I never once ran into trouble there. The fans in Neuilly absolutely loved us and we loved them.

I lived in a small house with two roommates in the heart of the 93; both boys were hockey players who had grown up in Montreal. We became instant brothers. We loved being able to take the RER subway into Paris on our days off. We visited the Eiffel Tower, the Louvre, and ate our lunches on the front lawns of cathedrals that were hundreds of years old. I loved getting lost in Paris's winding streets; I could sit for hours on the bridges over the river, just watching people and boats. I think that year in France was the most fun I've ever had with a hockey team anywhere. There were Slovak, Canadian, Finnish, and Czech players all together, and we spent our days laughing at nothing and everything. Even though it was serious professional hockey and our coaches demanded our best, we were like a group of kids playing on a frozen pond in Québec.

The travel bug that had bitten me in Sofia at age thirteen had gotten me for life. And it's a good thing too, because after a couple of years of solid playing in Paris, I was offered a contract with a respected team in Kazakhstan called HK Astana. Though I hated to leave France, I signed the offer almost immediately, certain that returning to the former Soviet Union would bring me one big step closer to the KHL, and with a lot of sweat and determination, one small step closer to the NHL.

Chapter 8

Across the World: Kazakhstan

AFTER SPENDING SUNDAY MORNINGS dipping crois-
sants in *café au lait* in Paris, Kazakhstan was quite a blow.
I arrived in the capital, Astana, with a suitcase full of warm
winter clothes and two giant bags of hockey equipment. I
remember thinking the people on the street all seemed to be
in a rush. Parts of the downtown were pretty, even under a
colourless sky, but outside the city centre I felt as though I'd
stepped into an old communist movie from the Soviet era.

The taxi driver didn't say more than a word to me
during the ride home from the airport. When we arrived
at the dormitories, I was surprised to see a metal gate bar-
ring the roadway, as though we were entering a prison. The
driver opened the trunk and dropped my bags outside an
old military building that was still covered in its original
green paint, most of it peeling. I looked around nervously,
almost expecting a government agent to come and con-
fiscate my passport. I wandered into the lobby and asked

Eliezer heads to an away game in Kazakhstan.
COURTESY OF THE SHERBATOV FAMILY

someone in Russian where the elevators were. At least I spoke the language.

He looked at me and laughed. I understood: no elevators. I collected my keys, climbed three flights of stairs with my hockey bags and turned the knob on a door hanging by one hinge. It opened slowly in a series of low-pitched creaks and groans. When I saw the room, I almost wished I hadn't. There were nicer prison cells. The bed was so narrow that my shoulders actually hung over the sides, and since the floor was uneven, it rocked back and forth until I stuffed t-shirts under the short leg. No question about it; my world was about to become very, very different.

Life with the HK Astana team was like being in the military, only on skates. All players had to obey a strict ten o'clock curfew at night, and if we didn't make it through the gates before then, we had to find another place to sleep. We trained every single day for four or five hours. We ate the same meals at the same time in the same green cafeteria. In the morning they gave us a bowlful of buckwheat porridge called *kasha* that smelled like it was a week old. It probably was. I couldn't tell the difference between the bread and the cheese, which could both break your teeth. Half of us were missing teeth anyway from hockey so it didn't really matter. The food was generally terrible, but when you exercise that much you'll eat anything. I started dreaming of *steak frites* from my favourite restaurant in Paris.

During training camp, the team was all business and all sweat. I liked it for one reason and one reason only: the level of playing. I learned to be more aggressive on the ice, Soviet style, and more aware of players' movements around me. Off the rink, we studied new formations and set plays that I had never seen before. I felt strong. I was confident I had found the team to push me to the KHL, which was always in the back of my mind.

Our first game of the season was scheduled a month after my arrival. I was changing in the dressing room and discussing strategy when a security guard approached our coach, who suddenly looked very confused. He called me over.

"Apparently there's someone here to see you, Elie."

"To see me?" I asked. "Who?" I didn't know a soul in Kazakhstan.

The coach threw his hands up in the air. "Do I know? Guard says there's a rabbi here to see you."

I looked at him like he had just grown a second head. "A rabbi?"

He didn't even have time to answer me. An Orthodox Jewish rabbi slipped past the security guard and into the team dressing room, where we were all still lacing our skates. "I'm looking for the new Israeli player," he yelled, though there was no reason to yell because you could have heard a pin drop in there. Most guys were just trying to keep a straight face. In his arms, the rabbi was holding two baked challahs, a sweet, braided bread that Jews eat on Shabbat and other holidays.

"That's me," I told him, wide-eyed. "Eliezer. I'm the Israeli."

The rabbi smiled and held up the two challahs. "Can you wash your hands for the blessing?" he asked. I was about to explain to him that I had five minutes before the game, but he didn't look like someone who was ready to listen to excuses. When a rabbi tells you to do something, you do it. I ran to a sink and washed as quickly as I could. "EAT!" he commanded. I sat down on the bench and started eating while Rabbi Shmuel talked about Jewish culture in Astana. "You know, Eliezer," he began, "Jews have been in Kazakhstan for hundreds of years...." I barely remember the rest; I could only nod every few seconds because my mouth was so full. My teammates had already left for warm-up on the ice, which was not a good sign. I devoured the two challahs as fast as I could, ripping off pieces like an animal. Finally I finished chewing and thanked him for the gift. That evening, my very first game, I scored two beautiful goals: one for each challah.

Eliezer and Rabbi Shmuel Karnoach in Kazakhstan
COURTESY OF THE SHERBATOV FAMILY

When we were all celebrating our win in the dressing room, the coach sat down beside me to congratulate me. "Eliezer," he said, "do you think the rabbi can bring more bread for the whole team next time?" To this day, I'm still not sure if he was kidding.

Rabbi Shmuel became a good friend to me in Kazakhstan. He was a very kind and thoughtful man who seemed to have an answer to everything that worried me, in life and in hockey. Even after I left Astana, I always went to visit him whenever I came back. He invited me to celebrate the end of Yom Kippur with his family and the Jewish community. I remember a huge table filled with wine and fruit and all the foods from home I missed so much. I still keep in touch with him today.

I made a few close friends during my years in Kazakhstan, but also faced my share of bullies. There were lots of big egos on those teams. Many were former NHL players who had come home to finish their careers, while others hadn't succeeded in North America and didn't know what else to do with their lives. Those men carried the weight of their NHL failures with them, wandering from one game to the next, unconcerned by the final scores. One player in particular made a lot of lives miserable, including mine. He was at least 230 pounds and a very heavy drinker. For some reason he decided I was going to be his target for a while; I was never sure what he had against me and I didn't ask. There had been some quiet anti-Semitism from Russian players in Kazakhstan, but I hadn't heard any directly from his mouth; I think he just needed to hate someone. He was a bit like the grade three bullies at school, lashing out at other kids without really understanding why himself. I let the majority of his insults go without so much as a word. For me, fighting is always a last resort, even on the ice. But one day during practice he went too far.

"Sherbatov," he said to me, "I'm going to break your jaw."

He meant it. My heart started to pound and I could feel the adrenaline burning in my veins. I was sick and tired of his aggression, and I wasn't afraid of players who were taller or heavier than me. Thanks to my brothers, my training in martial arts had prepared me to defend myself against anyone. I went to the locker room before him and took off my equipment. When he walked through the door I rushed at him and punched him square in the face, more than once; he tried to fight back a little, shifting his massive weight, but I got him in a body lock in less than a few seconds. He was helpless, partly from surprise. Other players came over to break up the fight, so I let him go. And then he did the strangest thing. He stood up from the locker room floor, wiped the blood from his face, checked to see if his teeth were still there, and held out his hand to shake mine. I looked at him like he had lost his mind. "I respect you," he said, offering his hand again.

I almost laughed. I must have had a wild look on my face because a teammate beside me gave me a nudge. "Do it," he whispered. I shook his hand reluctantly. I never heard another word from him after that; mostly we just ignored each other. It was the strangest hockey brawl of my career, but it earned me some peace, not to mention a little respect from my teammates.

My performance during my first year with HK Astana was steady enough to get me traded to an even better team in Kazakhstan, Beibarys Atyrau. I agreed to the contract on one condition: that they give me a real apartment. I was sick to death of living with termites, and I never wanted to see green paint again for the rest of my life. The team managers agreed and I moved into a slightly better building that was at least painted white. The best part was shopping and cooking my own meals, far away from buckwheat porridge.

Because I had more freedom, my teammates and I went out from time to time in the evenings. We celebrated our biggest wins by eating dumplings in our favourite Kazakh restaurant. One night, three of my friends got a little carried away and had too much to drink. The bartender was getting impatient and gave me a look; it was almost four in the morning and I needed to get the boys home before they fell asleep in their chairs. In Kazakhstan, if you need a ride, you just flag down a car on the road and settle on a price. I waved to a driver while trying to prop up three drunken men who probably weighed more than six hundred pounds put together. "Come on, boys," I told them, stuffing them into the back seat. I hopped in the front.

"Where to?" asked the driver. He barely looked at us. One by one, I dropped my friends off at home, carrying each one of them directly into their apartment and throwing them on the nearest couch, which wasn't easy. One guy landed on the floor, so I just left him there and threw a blanket on him. He was snoring even before I even closed the door. I dropped off the last one and jumped back into the front seat. We were about five minutes from my apartment when the driver spoke for the first time.

"How much did we say?" he asked.

I told him the price we had agreed on, sensing trouble. He shook his head. "Not enough. You made me wait for you."

I checked my wallet, which, looking back, was probably not a good idea. "That was what we settled on outside the bar," I told him.

"It's not enough," he said, raising his voice. I gave in; this wasn't a battle I willing to fight. "Fine, I'll pay a little more, all right?" Even though I didn't have money to spare, I proposed a few more *tenge* to our original price, assuming that would be the end of it. I could see we were approaching my neighbourhood. "I'll get out here," I told him, not wanting him to see where I lived. Instead of pulling over, he stepped on the accelerator and sped down the road. "What are you doing?" I yelled, watching my street disappear in the rear-view mirror. "You passed my building!"

He looked straight ahead and gripped the wheel with both hands. "You'll give me that money in your wallet," he said slowly. "And if you don't, I'll drive you somewhere to make you give it to me."

I was furious he had cornered me like that, and furious with myself for getting into the front seat instead of the back. "No," I responded, raising my voice to match his. "I'll give you what we agreed on, you understand?" I had to hold my ground. In a rage, he stepped on the gas again. We must have been travelling fifty kilometres an hour.

His eyes flashed in anger. "Fine. You don't want to pay?" He took one hand off the steering wheel and reached into his coat pocket, pulling out a knife. I had the terror of my life; the driver was one inch from me and clearly out of his mind.

I had to think fast. I could either fight a man with a knife or hurl myself out of a vehicle travelling at high speed. If I defended myself, the car would likely veer off the road and kill us both. I didn't hesitate more than a second; I opened the door and jumped out of the car, rolling across the sidewalk and down the roadside.

When James Bond throws himself out of a car it always works out fairly well for him. Bond just stands up at the end and doesn't have a scratch. But in real life, it's not quite

Eliezer greets fans of Beibarys Atyrau in Kazakhstan.
GEOMETRIA. REPRINTED WITH PERMISSION

so easy. When I finally stopped rolling, I picked myself up and checked for broken bones. I was hurting badly, but I could still move. I looked up and saw the car turning around, so I ran into a nearby hotel and hid. The staff in the lobby looked terrified of me. I didn't realize it at the time, but all my clothes were torn and I was covered in blood. It's almost funny when I think about it now; I must have looked like I'd been attacked by wild dogs when in fact I was an Israeli hockey player who had been mugged by some lunatic in a car. When I was sure the coast was clear, I made my way home on foot, half running and half limping in the cold. I wasn't going to risk flagging down another stranger ever again. First life lesson in Kazakhstan learned: always take the bus.

⚬⚬⚬

DESPITE MY STRUGGLES with madmen and bullies, it was in Kazakhstan that I really began to shine as a star forward. With 45 points in 53 games, the 2015-2016 hockey season started and finished like a firecracker for me. Our talents took Beibarys Atyrau to the playoffs, where I piled on another ten points, and eventually, to the championships. We won the Kazakhstan Cup, which was a gift for my future. I knew the KHL was within my reach. I began to network more aggressively, hoping to attend a KHL training camp in a city which wasn't too deep into the icy heart of Russia. Kazakhstan was cold enough.

A few weeks after the championships I was finally invited to a tryout with Dinamo Riga, a KHL team based in Latvia. What started out as butterflies on the plane turned into a slow-burning panic in the hours before my first practice. At first I managed to score a couple of goals in team scrimmages, but as the days passed I became more and more overwhelmed, not by the level of playing, but by my own thoughts and uncertainty. My game deteriorated quickly. I remember sitting on the bench between shifts with trembling hands, desperate to find a way to turn things around. When the general manager refused to sign me, I wasn't surprised.

Though I returned to Kazakhstan feeling defeated, it didn't take long for the fighter in me to resurface; I became utterly determined to prove Dinamo Riga had made a mistake. I did belong in the KHL, I was sure of it. That very

Eliezer sports a playoff beard and raises the Kazakhstan Cup with Beibarys Atyrau in 2016. OLGA KOROTKOVA FOR SHAIBA.KZ, KAZAKHSTAN HOCKEY FEDERATION. REPRINTED WITH PERMISSION

next season in Kazakhstan, sheer will drove me to a stellar performance with 43 points in 46 games. And the press and game commentators were loving the show.

"As usual Eliezer jumps on the ice with his wild eyes," sang one broadcaster, "and scores a beautiful goal. And there you have it: 2-0. No chance for the other team."

"On Eliezer's planet," cried another, "everyone should play that kind of hockey. In the Italian soccer league, they call those kinds of players *fantasistas*."

I loved all the attention, but *fantasista* or not, what I needed most was to be invited to another KHL tryout. I spent the summer months of 2017 in Montreal, training, networking, and hoping, and with the help of my child-hood friend and former NHL defenseman Simon Després, we both received contract offers from Slovan Bratislava, a KHL team based in Slovakia. In a matter of hours, we signed on the dotted line, shook our agent's hand, and rushed to the airport, hoping to arrive on time for our first regulation game. I was off on yet another hockey journey in yet another country, chasing my dream of becoming the first Israeli in the KHL. This is it, I remember think-ing, watching Montreal's lights disappear from my plane window. It's now or never.

Chapter 9

The KHL

BRATISLAVA WAS BEAUTIFUL CITY right on the river Danube. I shared a two-floor apartment with Simon in the Old Town, surrounded by cafés, ancient churches, and boutiques with wonderful breads and cheeses. I came to know some of the local shopkeepers, who saved me slices of their best cakes. Christmastime was my favourite. Everybody drank traditional hot wine and wandered along the river, which was lit by tiny white lights on every building. I was a long way from Kazakhstan.

My first appearance in the KHL was complicated by some bad timing. I hadn't been invited early enough to participate in training camp, so the coaches weren't even sure what I was capable of. Even worse, the Slovan team roster was actually full, so I had to fight for a spot that didn't even exist yet. I had agreed to a two-way contract, which meant that if I didn't perform at a high enough level, I would be demoted to the minor league team affiliated with Slovan Bratislava. I was determined to make it work. I played my heart out in practice, making sure the coaches saw the best of me, especially my speed and puck handling. They agreed to give me a chance.

I was jittery before my first game, panicked even. It was a test, my one and only shot at a career in the big leagues. I was also still a bit intimidated by the former NHL players wandering all over the dressing room. I took off my brace quickly on the bench and stuffed it in my locker; I didn't have the strength or patience to answer any of the usual questions. With the exception of Simon, I didn't know the team and I knew next to nothing about their set plays and strategies. I was going on the rink cold.

A few hours before the buzzer sounded, the coaches decided I would play on the third line, which meant that my role was more defensive than anything else. Our job was to stop the other team's best players from scoring, which was going to be a huge challenge for me. I had been a first-line forward my whole life, either a left winger or a centre. In my heart, I'm all about scoring. I feed off the crowd. I need them to make me feel alive, to inspire me, to push through those extra few seconds in a shift when I'm sure I have no strength left. When I score, I like to celebrate with a brief slide across the rink on my knees, just to make the fans happy. Some players like it, others don't, but that never really mattered to me. Without fans, I doubt I would have lasted as long as I did. Hearing them scream, cheer, chant, and curse—I love it all.

Which is why I was thrilled to play for 11,000 fans on home ice in Bratislava. As luck would have it, our very first game was against Dinamo Riga, the Latvian team that

Eliezer and former NHL defenseman Simon Després brave
the KHL together. COURTESY OF THE SHERBATOV FAMILY

had refused to sign me. It was quite a crowd. I had about
ten minutes to figure out how to play defensively against
the best competitors I had ever faced. I decided to be the
person I had always been: a fast and energetic player who
draws in the crowd.

I buzzed around the rink like a fly, picking up the puck
here, passing it there. The fans loved it. After I made a particularly good play, the crowd briefly chanted my name. It
was music to my ears and to the team manager's too. If
you can rile up the fans, it sells seats. The coaches decided

to keep me on the team roster and actually fired a Finnish player to make room for me on the bench. It was official: I was the first Israeli to play in the KHL, and I was proud.

As the season progressed, being on the third line proved to be more difficult than I had hoped; in my head I believed it was all about stopping goals rather than scoring them. Since I was terrified of giving up the puck in our end, I rarely ventured deep into the opposing team's side where I could score. Eventually, though, I became a decent defender, and the coaches seemed satisfied. Unfortunately, it didn't show in my statistics. Ten games later I had yet to score a goal, and I had no idea how to make it happen.

Playing in the KHL meant a ton of travel. The twenty-five teams are located all over Europe and Asia, but most are in Russia. About two months into the season, Slovan headed to what might have been the end of the earth, to a region called Yugra. It was smack in the middle of Siberia, a desert filled with ice. The cold in Yugra cut through me like a knife. Tears froze almost instantly, never quite making it down our cheeks. Everything in Yugra was white, the air, our breath, the view from our hotel windows; it was difficult to see anything at all because there was so much blowing snow. I stared out at the emptiness and asked my teammate where the woolly mammoths were. It was another world, another era. I went to the arena feeling first overwhelmed, and then amazed to see long lines of fans wandering into the building like ghosts appearing out of the night.

We were scheduled to play in a town called Khanty-Mansiysk, about 2,600 kilometres east of Moscow, my family's first home. Our game started with the routine national anthems and we all stood silently on the ice to listen. The Russian anthem echoed through the arena with all its glory, fanfare, trumpets, and crashing cymbals. I was suddenly overwhelmed with emotion. I thought of my parents, of my grandparents, and of all the Jews who had been forced to leave a nation that we could have loved, but that didn't love us. I wasn't at all unhappy; I simply breathed in that moment and remembered them. What a time for me, I thought, who had dreamed of playing in the KHL, and who was finally here. *Just enjoy it*, I told myself. *Enjoy the game and play for all the people who love you and who carried you here.*

That night, I found my wings for the first time in months. I remembered the forward I used to be and scored what would be my first and only goal in the KHL. I slid across the ice on one knee to celebrate. After seven years of professional hockey, who could blame me?

I played thirty-five games with Slovan in 2017-2018, and despite my statistics and our disastrous finish in the KHL standings, the organisation seemed willing to renew my contract. The problem was that for the entire year I hadn't been paid, nor had many of my teammates. I actually played those thirty-five games for free. Because of mismanagement, the team and coaches were in chaos, and I was broke. I learned a few months later that the entire KHL was having financial troubles that year. They finally eliminated two full teams to cut back on players' salaries, one of them from Yugra, where I had scored my first goal. As much as I loved the KHL, Bratislava was not the place to be.

What I really wanted, most of all, was to be invited to an NHL tryout. I flew back to Montreal and asked my agent to convince the general manager of the Canadiens to let me participate in their September training camp. It was my childhood team, my family's team, and in many ways, the reason my father had chosen to bring us all to Montreal. It didn't seem impossible. Television reporters visited me at my gym and did an interview about the Canadiens giving me a chance. "I played in the KHL," I told them. "Now I'm ready to break into the NHL. I'm close, I can feel it." I was happy to see articles appearing online too: *Will Eliezer Sherbatov be invited to the Canadiens' training camp?* I checked my cellphone constantly, willing it to ring.

I networked as best I could, but in the end, it didn't happen. The general manager of the Canadiens did finally speak with my agent and confirm—I'd like to think regret-fully—that there was just no room on the team for another winger. The training camp came and went without me, and I had to resign myself to watching my favourite team on television with the rest of Québec. It left me feeling empty. Disoriented even.

In the weeks that followed my mood became dark. It was as though my eight-year journey through professional hockey had somehow all been meaningless. What was it all for? I didn't even know anymore. In all my dreams I had imagined myself in the Canadiens' red and blue jersey, playing on home ice for my parents and brothers, and that dream was finally over. I decided to try to return to a team in the KHL, but nothing panned out.

The letdown of being not quite good enough for the Canadiens began a strange and unpredictable year that sent me to four different countries: from Montreal I went to Latvia, France, Kazakhstan, and Slovakia, where I played just a few games with every team, looking for the right fit and the right contract. I spent more time in airplanes than I did on the ice. I was frustrated with everything and everyone, and at times, I felt hopeless. A small part of me wondered if I should just give up hockey and return to Montreal, where Somaly and my family were waiting for me. But at the end of those months of drifting, I had one brief light: I was free to join the Israeli national team for the World Hockey Championships in Mexico City. It was a relief to come back to a familiar tournament and play for the country I loved so much.

Since my very first appearance in Sofia at age thirteen, I had played for Israel whenever my schedule allowed it. I missed just a few years when I was in Kazakhstan. The team's performance had been up and down; we always seemed to be moving between Division II and III, which meant our skills were somewhere in the middle. In 2019, we were facing opponents in Division IIB and needed to be at our absolute best to stay there. I didn't dare think of being promoted.

I flew to Mexico and reconnected with the team; some of the younger players were new, while others were close friends I had played with for years. We had two powerful forwards, Evgeni Kozhevnikov, who had spent his career in Germany before coming to Israel, and veteran left wing Sergei Frenkel. The players all looked strong. During our first team meeting, the assistant coach, Ron Oz, asked me to come to the front of the room. I was surprised.

I had known Ron for years; we had played together as teammates on the Israeli national team when I was still a teenager. He shook my hand, smiling. "You've always been with us, Elie, ever since you were thirteen, and we're grateful for your skills. You've been a real ambassador to Israel everywhere you've ever played. So…" He picked up a jersey from the table and handed it to me. "We've chosen you as the team captain for 2019."

All the boys clapped and banged on the table with their fists. The jersey had my name on the back, with the "C" stitched on the front. It was an honour for me, especially since I'd been absent the last few years. I felt a huge sense of responsibility too. I remembered how my own team captain had promised he would protect me during my first World Championship tournament in Sofia, when I was so small I could barely see over the boards. I had to find a way to that gold medal for Israel. It was up to me to make my team believe we could win and to make them play the best hockey of their lives. There were just two very, very big obstacles in my way: altitude and Mexican water.

I made a grave error on my second day in Mexico: I ate vegetables that had been washed in contaminated water. I had assumed food was all carefully prepared for us, but I was sorely mistaken. Needless to say, I got sick. Really sick.

I wasn't even sure I could play in the tournament at all until the team physiotherapist took matters into his own hands. He fed me heaps of powdered charcoal to absorb the toxins. My mouth, teeth, and face were black; I was completely covered in soot. Exhausted, I washed as best I could and crawled into bed, unsure of what the morning held.

I felt like I was sleepwalking the next day, but as team captain, I was determined to play our first game against Iceland. That was when I faced my second surprise, and it wasn't good. Even though I had travelled all over the world, I had never competed in a city with the altitude of Mexico City. In Slovakia, where I had been prior to the tournament, the altitude is 200 metres. In Mexico City, it's 2,250 metres. Those extra 2,000 metres make it difficult to breathe, let alone skate. Which is why the tournament organizers supplied three oxygen tanks right beside the team bench. When the game against Iceland began, I realized those tanks were my going to be my new best friends.

A normal shift on the ice is about 45 seconds to a minute. In Mexico, I could only last ten seconds before I had to rush back to the bench and gulp oxygen like a ninety-year-old man. I couldn't believe how hard it was to move, to accelerate, even to shoot. Between the upset stomach and the altitude, I was a disaster on skates.

It was the team that saved me. That saved us. The 2019 Israeli team, they had talent and heart. They saw their captain falling apart and they stepped up their game. We won our first match against Iceland 6-3, and I didn't

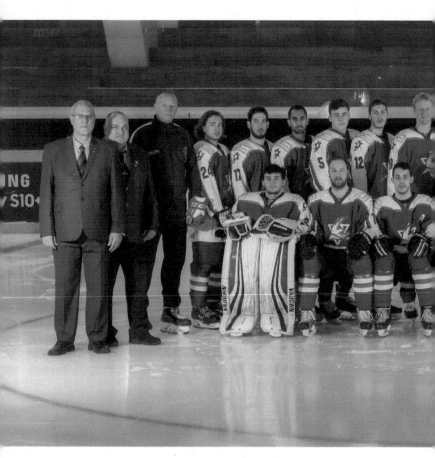

Fourteen years after Eliezer's first appearance in Bulgaria, Israel wins
gold in Division IIB of the World Hockey Championships in 2019.
Eliezer is seated in the centre with the "C" on his jersey.

ISRAEL HOCKEY FOUNDATION OF NORTH AMERICA

REPRINTED WITH PERMISSION

score a single goal. I was so proud of them; it really was
a team victory that gave us the confidence we all needed.
After that, the wins just didn't stop. New Zealand, North
Korea, Mexico, and Georgia all lost to us one by one, and

we claimed the gold medal for Israel. I think I recovered so quickly physically because of the way my teammates were performing; my mind just refused to let them down, even if my body had.

In the end, I bounced back to become the tournament's lead goal scorer with fifteen points in five games. I credit every one of those points to the team. That gold medal— and I've had more than a few—is the one I'm most proud of.

It brought me back to that little kid who had won bronze at age thirteen in Sofia. In a way, I had come full circle.

Israel was promoted to Division IIA for 2020, but of course the tournament was cancelled due to the pandemic. When we finally arrived at the 2022 World Championships, we were all more than a little rusty after the long break. Let's just say the games didn't go quite as we planned. But you can bet Israel will be back next year, leaving it all on the ice, as we always do.

Chapter 10

Ghosts

AFTER THE CHAOS of playing in five countries in 2018-2019, I wanted a steady hockey contract in one city. I decided to return to Kazakhstan for one season and give it my all. All that sweat and determination helped me finish the year as one of the best goal-scorers in the league, with 55 points in 49 games. Though I loved the team and especially the fans, outside the arena, things were more complicated. For one, I was living in terrible conditions again, even worse than before; my room in Pavlodar almost made the dormitories in Astana look like a five-star hotel. The building's elevator was terrifying too. The floor was just a few pieces of wood that had been nailed together, so I could actually see the insides of the elevator shaft below. I imagined myself plummeting down to the bottom and having to scale my way out by tying my hockey equipment into a rope. Even worse, the building was filled with insects. Enough was enough. I was twenty-seven years old, and I wanted some semblance of a comfortable life. I called my agent and asked him to search for a contract where I could live well and ask Somaly to join me.

Somaly and I had been in different countries for the better part of eight years, but we knew we wanted to be together forever. I had loved her ever since I was sixteen years old. Before I left for Kazakhstan, we learned that we were expecting our first child. Being the romantic that I am, I surprised Somaly by getting down on one knee and asking her to marry me. I planned it for weeks, with flowers and champagne and tons of food, surrounded by all the family we loved in Montreal. Lucky for me, she said yes.

My beautiful daughter, Louna, was born in February of 2020, while I was still playing hockey in Kazakhstan. I wasn't present for her birth and desperately wanted to get home, but I was tied to my contract. It didn't matter though; one month later, the pandemic arrived and the world seemed to stop spinning. The government announced that European borders were closing, which terrified me. I realized that if I didn't move quickly, I would be trapped in Pavlodar. I had to find a way home. I was not going to spend the next months of my life alone in a room full of beetles.

I paid a taxi to drive me over four hundred kilometres across the border to Omsk, Russia, where I hoped to find a flight to Europe. I carried my life with me: a huge hockey bag, hockey sticks, a suitcase, a carry on, and a backpack. Even though it was freezing outside, I was sweating the entire way, only half listening to the driver's conversation. We arrived at the border after nightfall, so the temperature had plunged to minus twenty. The guard looked into the taxi and shook his head. "No vehicles can pass."

I handed him my Russian passport, hoping it would save me. "I'm a Russian citizen," I told him. "I'm going home. Please. I have to get to the airport. I have five bags with me."

"*Nyet*," he answered, shaking his head. "It's not allowed. You can go, but you have to walk through. There are taxis on the Russian side to take you to the airport." His face was like stone.

I looked through the window at the long, icy kilometre that separated me from the airport and from my new family in Montreal. I pulled down my hat and arranged my equipment as best I could on my back and shoulders. The wind was so strong that I had to lean forward to walk, falling a couple of times under the weight of my bags. I kept my eye on the lights of the border crossing so I wouldn't veer off the road and disappear into the night. When I finally stumbled into Russia, my beard was covered in ice. I couldn't stop shivering, even in the taxi. And to make matters worse, the airport kiosk in Omsk was closed for another few hours. I just lay down on my hockey bags and slept right there on the dirty floor.

In the early morning I booked a flight to Moscow and then to New York City, where I waited again for a connecting flight to Montreal. I travelled for more than thirty-six hours straight, wary of every stranger I met along the way. Even at home it was many days before I could be near Somaly and my new baby; I was afraid of giving them the virus from my journey. I could only look at Louna from across the room and try and make her smile. When Somaly finally put my daughter in my arms, I was so relieved and happy that I just sat down and cried. It was and always will be the best day of my life. Louna, I found myself thinking, don't you dare grow up too soon.

∞

THOUGH THE PANDEMIC HAD STOPPED THE WORLD, it also allowed me to slow down and live quietly for a while without the pressures of hockey. I spent months just enjoying being a father to the happiest little girl. Still, I knew it wouldn't last forever, and I needed to find another hockey contract to support my new family. I wanted to live in a city that was safe and comfortable for a baby; Somaly and Louna were planning to join me wherever I chose to go. I was not going to miss the first year of my daughter's life.

I contacted my old teammate and friend, Klemen Pretnar, and asked where he was playing. Klemen was a talented defenseman and I admired him. He was a real journeyman in his hockey years, moving all over Europe to play. He mentioned the name of a city in Poland I had never heard of: Oswiecim. He said he had been generally happy there; the team was strong and the fans loved them because it was such a sleepy town. With Klemen's help, the team manager made me an offer, which I originally refused because it wasn't enough money to support my family. I still hadn't fully realized where exactly I was trying to go

Eliezer holds Louna for the first time, at home in Montreal.

in Poland. During negotiations with the manager, the way he pronounced the name of the town made me stop in my tracks. I suddenly understood that Oswiecim was in fact the Polish name for the town the world called Auschwitz, where one million Jews had been murdered in a concentration camp during the Second World War. I put my head in my hands, stunned by the realization.

My first instinct was to refuse the contract, but it didn't seem right in my heart. I needed advice. I called my parents and told them about the offer, unsure of what to expect.

Some of my father's relatives had died in concentration camps, and I knew his perspective was an important one. My parents' reaction astonished me. They were happy.

"Go," said my father. "Go and face the past and remember it for all of us. Show the world the strength of the Jewish people. Go as an Israeli and show your lion's heart. I'm so proud of you, Eliezer. You make us even prouder."

"Maybe," said my mother, "God chose you for this task."

I felt overwhelmed by the choice I was about to make. I wouldn't have had the strength to go to Poland without the support of my family. Somaly felt the same as my parents and promised to be by my side when I needed her most. I left for Poland in July of 2020, with Somaly making plans to follow in the fall. I would face my first months in Oswiecim alone.

My decision to play in Auschwitz resulted in a shocking media storm. I was used to hockey interviews after a game, but before my departure I was thrown into a frenzy of cameras and lights, microphones, and social media, and it continued in Poland too. I had always had a social media presence and loved posting silly videos of friends and family, but this was all new to me because the questions were so personal and the answers so complicated. My phone rang all day. Israeli and French reporters called, Americans, Canadians, Russians. Everyone wanted to know why a proud Israeli who had represented his country from the age of thirteen would choose to wear a jersey with Oswiecim across his chest. The headlines were everywhere: *Israel's national hockey captain has joined a team based in the same town as Auschwitz*; *Israeli hockey player in hot water for signing with team Auschwitz; Jewish hockey player addresses backlash after signing with team Auschwitz.* It was endless. I tried to explain my decision as best I could, speaking English, French, and Russian; no language seemed to have the right words to express what I believed, or why I had chosen this path. I began to repeat myself mechanically during interviews, unsure if the world understood.

I was greeted at the Krakow airport and driven to our new apartment, which was pretty both inside and out. Oswiecim was quite a beautiful place. There were birch trees everywhere and the sky swirled a piercing blue. White swans were living on the riverbanks nearby, and I thought about feeding them with Louna in the mornings. I felt briefly reassured, slightly less unsteady, but that feeling didn't last.

What I was not prepared for was the proximity of the death camp to the city, and to our own apartment. Auschwitz was only five minutes from cafés, from grocery stores, and from the hockey rink. It was impossible to comprehend. I was stunned that I could actually see its buildings in the distance from my apartment window. Even today I cannot find the words to describe my emotions the moment I realized what I was looking at. My thoughts went immediately to my daughter. I wasn't sure the first year of her life should be spent in Oswiecim, a town overwhelmed by its own devastating history.

I thought about visiting the camp by myself before the hockey season started but couldn't find the courage. Every structure and every place in Oswiecim felt haunted to me; the walls, the rooms, the train tracks that barely separated the city from the death camp. The earth and the grass seemed sacred because of what lay beneath it. The waters of the river Sola, filled with swans, were also flowing with ashes. An old college nearby had actually been home to women who were members of the SS, the German police that terrorized Jews and sent them to their deaths. There were students in that same building now, coming and going with biology and math textbooks. It was astonishing to see something so routine, so normal, in a place that was once so utterly evil. There were ghosts everywhere in Oswiecim and they followed me for months.

What happened next was heartbreaking for me. A rabbi decided to use social media to label me a traitor to my homeland. "For a Jew to play for team Auschwitz is treason," he wrote, "a betrayal of the Jewish people, and a shameful stab in the back for millions." I was stunned that my actions had been so misinterpreted. At first I was angry, but then I remembered why I had come. I knew my reasons to be true. I also came to realize that he was entitled to his opinion; he had a different history, different pain, and we were different people. I tweeted a response, asking him to understand that my decision was much bigger than us both. I wanted to move forward, to move towards something better. I think, that in the end, most people understood that. Overall, I received much more support than I did criticism. A thousand times more from the Polish people, from whom I never once heard a negative word.

I needed to remember why I had come to Poland: to play hockey. I needed to overcome my doubts and remember my father's words. I had so many reminders of why life was good. Somaly, my mother, and Louna were arriving in October, and I was being paid to do what I loved. I desperately wanted a distraction from my surroundings and the constant media attention. More than ever, I *needed* to play hockey.

The rink in Oswiecim seated more than two thousand fans, but for my first game, it sounded like there were twenty thousand. The town was so sleepy, I really hadn't expected so much noise from the crowd. The minute the announcer said my name and I stepped on the ice, the arena absolutely exploded. In some ways I think the locals of Oswiecim saw me as a way to distance themselves from the darkness that haunted them all and would likely haunt their children and their grandchildren. My arrival had driven the smallest of wedges between them and the past and they were grateful.

Before the game, I took a moment to tap my two tattoos for luck. One is a Star of David, and the other is a red circle on my wrist to ward off the evil eye, an old Jewish superstition. Hockey players all have little rituals before a game; goalies like to touch the three sides of the doorway before they go on the rink. It turned out that I didn't need to worry about bad luck that night. I was so fired up, so emotional, all of it came out on the ice. I scored my first goal and had one assist for a two-point game. When I celebrated the goal, I did it for Israel. I didn't forget where I was. I couldn't.

I played well during my months in Poland, managing 26 points in 35 games. Still, when it came time to consider

Eliezer, Somaly, and Louna in Poland
COURTESY OF THE SHERBATOV FAMILY

staying for a second season, there were just too many complications, and contract negotiations ended badly. A few months into the year, I also discovered that my teammates had taken a pay cut in order to bring me to Poland. I hadn't known when I signed. It created some tension in the dressing room, and I know the team was sick to death of the cameras and journalists who were always knocking on the door to interview me. When Covid finally hit Poland hard, the fans disappeared entirely and we played for empty arenas in silence. Eventually games stopped all together. It was a terrible time, for all of us.

When the fans left the stands, I think my heart did too. Somaly and I missed our families, and we knew our parents were desperate to be with their newest grandchild. The hockey season finally ended in March due to the pandemic, so we packed up our lives and our little girl and went home to Montreal. I never did visit Auschwitz. I had intended to go with an Israeli camera crew, but as the pandemic spread, travel became more and more restricted and the plan was eventually cancelled. In truth, I was relieved. I realized that I didn't want my experience there to be filmed, becoming permanent for all the world to see. And I didn't even know if I could handle seeing the camp without my parents' support. How do you confront what you can never understand?

I'm not disappointed in myself. I felt the weight of history more than I ever had that year. It's enough to have lived where I lived, to have breathed what I breathed, and to have played where I played. All of it was enough.

Chapter 11

An Unexpected War

OF ALL THE PLACES IN THE WORLD, I started the 2021 season with a team in Ukraine, where my great-grandfather was born. Mariupol is a grey, industrial city on the sea of Azov, and a sour smell of pollution and salt often fills the air. Though I loved my teammates and was proud to be named Assistant Captain, my first few months abroad were uneventful and quiet. Mostly I was lonely. There was a small park with playground equipment near my apartment building, and every child's laugh reminded me of Louna, who was growing like a weed and speaking her first words of French and Russian. My son, Tuvia, was born in November in Montreal, and I of course couldn't be home for his birth, so my heart ached to see him. Somaly and I had decided it would be best for them to stay in Québec, where grandparents would always be there to lend a hand. It was a difficult decision for us both, and as the months passed, living apart became harder and harder.

The rumours of a Russian invasion started circulating in the late fall of 2021. Like everyone else in my city, I believed that war was impossible, and that despite the hundreds of tanks amassing at Ukrainian borders, the reports were exaggerated, or Putin was simply displaying his military might to the West. "It's been like this for years," people told me. "Always the same. It will pass." Nothing changed in those cold winter months; people shopped in grocery stores, children went to the park, and the team played hockey. Life continued as it always had. Every time someone spoke of war, people simply shook their heads and dismissed it. On New Year's Eve we raised a glass to our futures while Russian troops continued to quietly surround the country.

Seven weeks later, the team travelled to an away game in Druzhkivka, a small town about two hundred kilometres north of Mariupol. We still felt relatively safe; the team manager had promised he would evacuate us immediately if there was any movement into Ukrainian territory. An invasion would advance slowly, we thought, foreigners could make their way to the borders, and civilians would be spared. How wrong we all were. Now that I am distanced from it, I understand that war is often like that; people simply believe that there is humanity and compassion, and that no army, no man, would ever be so evil as to raise his gun to an innocent person. War is impossible to comprehend until you're in it.

In the early morning of February 24th, three explosions rocked us from our hotel beds in Druzhkivka. A black sky was lit by swelling flashes of light as missiles struck the earth, one after another. Our walls shook. Because they were followed by complete silence, we still didn't truly comprehend what had happened until we all gathered for a team meeting in the dining room.

"The war has begun," our coach told us, his face white. "We advise you to stay here and take refuge in the hotel. Moving through the country is incredibly dangerous, but it's your choice. I can't stop you."

My breath caught in my chest. It was as though I wasn't really there, as though I wasn't truly hearing him say the words he was speaking. Everyone picked up a cellphone and started dialing. Somewhere within myself, I found the strength to focus on what needed to be done, and quickly. I contacted the Canadian government by phone and email, asking them what to do and where to go, but my pleas for help were all met with silence and automatic replies. I became more desperate. I spoke briefly on the phone with journalists I knew in Canada to tell them about my situation, hoping it might help bring me home faster. Friends alerted the Israeli embassy and gave them my contact information. I was overwhelmed with emotion when I reached a representative almost immediately. A human voice. "Get out of there," he told me. "If you can get to the western city of Lviv, there are Israeli volunteers who can help you reach the Polish border. Just get out *now*." Tanks rolled in front of the hotel while we spoke, whether they were Ukrainian or Russian, I didn't know.

I couldn't think. I could only pace up and down the halls like an animal, and if I sat down, I became so agitated that I had to immediately stand up to go to a different room. My body felt heavy as I moved, almost weighted to the earth, as though I was being buried alive by time. Sometimes I sat in silence with my trainer, Sergei, who was able to calm me down. Some of my teammates drank whiskey in their rooms and covered the windows with mattresses, while others stayed in the corridors because they claimed it was the safest place, protected between two walls. I couldn't even look at them, and if I did, I looked right through them. My emotions shifted from despair to rage.

I had one glimmer of hope that Thursday night. Deniss Berdniks, a Latvian defenseman in my league, came to the hotel in search of shelter from Kramatorsk, which was under Russian siege. He was desperate to flee to the west of the country. We sat down together with two others who also had foreign citizenship: my close friend and centre on my line, Vlad, and the team doctor, Roman.

"We're across from the train station," said Deniss. "We have to find out if trains are still running. We need to have options. We need to have tickets."

"We can't just sit here waiting to die," I told them. "The war will only get worse from here. And we have no bomb shelter."

If there were four of us, I felt I would at least have support, someone to help me if I was hurt. And that was all I truly had. My backpack held $100, my toothbrush, water, two chocolate bars, my hockey jersey, and my passports. Everything else was still in my apartment in Mariupol, forever lost to me. No one could withdraw money because bank machines everywhere were emptied of cash.

The next morning was quiet in Druzhkivka. The four of us made our way to the train station on foot and reserved some of the last tickets for the only train to Lviv, scheduled to depart in the late afternoon. We returned to the hotel to wait. I felt hopeful. I had a chance, a window; I had to take it.

While we were preparing to leave for the station, Vlad received a phone call from a Ukrainian friend in the military. "If you board the next train," she told him, her voice breaking, "there is a fifty percent chance you won't make it. Trains are being gunned down." I could hear her crying.

Vlad looked at us, the colour draining from his face. "I can't do it," he whispered. "I just can't do it. I don't want to die. Go without me. Go." He took off his winter coat and left the room.

I felt everything inside me implode. What was worse? To take a train into the heart of the war, or to stay and face thirst and hunger, a missile, a fire, or the collapse of buildings onto a bomb shelter, if I could even find one? I began to play a sickening game of math in my head, trying to calculate the risks involved, reducing my own life to numbers. I was terrorised by thoughts of my children growing up without me. Finally I called my father, who has guided me in every decision I have ever made.

"Dad," I asked him, sweat and tears on my face, "what

should I do?" I grasped onto my telephone with two hands to stop it from shaking.

For a moment there was a terrible silence; my father understood the enormity of the words he was about to say. Finally he spoke. "If the train comes, Eliezer," he said, "it's because God wants you to get on that train. If it comes, take it. Take it, Elie."

I hung up the phone quickly, wishing I'd thought to tell him I loved him, and went in search of my teammates to say my goodbyes. A few of them tried again to persuade me to stay but I held up my hands; I just couldn't bear to listen to it anymore. All I knew was that I had to get on that train. On my way out the door I overheard someone talking quietly to Vlad. "You made the right decision," he whispered. "They're going to die." I stopped for a brief moment, paralyzed by his words. I turned my head slightly and met Sergei's gaze, my trainer who had taken care of me and been like a father to all of us. He nodded his head silently, telling me to go, telling me it would be all right, telling me he would be praying for me. I nodded back at him and left.

The train arrived four hours late, at nine o'clock at night. Since Druzhkivka was the second stop, it was still mostly empty. It was an old Soviet sleeper train, so there were no seats, only four beds crowded into a small compartment with a door. Deniss and I said goodbye to Roman, who entered a railcar further back, and found an empty compartment for the two of us. I sipped a little water with trembling hands; in the next eight hours we would be passing directly through lines of fire in Kramatorsk, Kharkiv and Kyiv, all cities under Russian siege. We travelled in complete darkness with the blinds drawn so the faintest of lights wouldn't alert the Russians. Every few minutes I would look over at Deniss and say the same four words. "Are you all right?"

"Yes, yes," he answered. "You?"

"Yes," I lied. "I'm fine. We're fine."

I have never felt so alone in my life as I did on that train. When we approached Kharkiv, a city of over a million people, we could hear faraway sounds of shelling. I was horrified to see train platforms crowded with women, children, and elderly people, all of them standing in the cold. The train's doors opened and hundreds of people pushed their way inside, packing the aisles. I opened the door of our compartment to let them in and heard French voices. "*Entrez, entrez*," I told them. A group of four Moroccan students and a Ukrainian man piled into the tiny room with all their luggage. Two nineteen-year-old women crouched on the floor outside our door, but I told them to come in. That was all we could fit without someone being crushed. The train had hundreds more people than it should, all of them exhausted and hungry. In a matter of hours, the air became thick and stifling and reeked of sweat.

Though there were muted voices throughout the train in daylight, at night we all sat silently, as though a single movement could attract the war outside. When we approached Kyiv I was shaking so badly that I had to wrap my arms around myself. Nobody spoke. I felt the weight of the train shift as the doors opened and a flood of people tried to

A man lies in the aisle of Eliezer's train en route to Lviv, a city in the west of Ukraine. COURTESY OF THE SHERBATOV FAMILY

make their way on board, hoping to save themselves and their children. I pressed my forehead against the wall and closed my eyes.

After almost two hours in Kyiv the train left the station, heading towards unthreatened territory in the west of the country. Every mile we advanced felt like a victory. I began to breathe slowly, to come back to myself, and even spoke with the strangers in my compartment, our lives now connected through the shock of war and the relief of surviving it. I gave my last sixty dollars to the Ukrainian women so they could buy something to eat in Lviv; they had nothing with them but clothes.

We pulled into the Lviv train station dirty and exhausted, twenty-four hours after we had left Druzhkivka. My body ached from sitting and from dehydration, but we had to move quickly; we needed to locate the Israeli consulate, which was operating out of a business to help citizens and Jewish Ukrainians to safety. We fought our way into the train station and into the chaos of bodies everywhere; almost everyone was screaming into a telephone in order to be heard, holding up cardboard signs with people's names scribbled on them, or searching for a way to reach the Polish border. Eighty kilometres separated Lviv from Poland, and thousands of desperate families were making the trip on foot, some carrying children.

An acquaintance of Deniss's picked us up at the station and drove us to the Israeli consulate, where we ate for the first time in days and washed in the sink as best we could. After we'd been briefed on the next leg of the trip and were preparing to leave, the Israeli coordinator asked to speak with me.

"Listen," he said. "We can't go with you; there are more Israeli citizens coming. After the bus drops you off, I need you to take people across the border and into Poland. I'm putting you in charge of this group. Understand?"

I must have nodded, because he kept talking.

"You have to keep them together," he said, almost yelling. "That's your job. You can't let anyone leave, not even for a moment. No one can go to the bathroom without all of you going to the bathroom, you understand?" He pointed at my chest. "There are seventeen others, mainly women, children, and elderly, and it's your responsibility to get every single one of them to the Israeli embassy in

Warsaw. Once an hour, you take a five second video of the group and email it to journalists in Israel, so we can track your location. Charge your phone."

I swallowed hard. I had been thinking only of my own survival for three days; I couldn't even imagine seventeen other lives. "I understand," I told him. "I'll get them there."

Since we refused to be separated, the consulate agreed to let Deniss travel with us, even though he wasn't Jewish or a citizen of Israel. For this and so much else, I will never forget them. The checkpoints along the way were endless; every few miles we were stopped by Ukrainian soldiers who interrogated us and demanded our passports. I spoke only my best English, never Russian, out of fear they would associate me with their aggressors or turn me away. In fact, I had hidden my Russian passport at the bottom of my backpack.

The Ukrainian border was a scene I will remember for the rest of my life. There was an ocean of people, thousands of them standing in long lines in the mud, some eating or sleeping, some crying, some trying to warm themselves around small fires that had been lit to prevent frostbite. The bus left us there at night and returned to Lviv to pick up more passengers. We found a place at the end of a line for elderly people and children and stood close to one another for warmth. At one point the guards tried to separate us and force the men into a different line, but we all fought back. In the ten hours it took us to cross into Poland, I focused on keeping the group together and nothing else. We went to the bathroom once only, at a gas station along the highway, all eighteen of us.

Eliezer's makeshift armband, identifying him as an Israeli citizen
COURTESY OF THE SHERBATOV FAMILY

The Polish side of the border was another sea of refugees, buses, and chaos. The Red Cross was there, armed guards, volunteers from every nation distributing food, water, blankets, and toys, and people sleeping against one another out of exhaustion. The children in our group visited the food tables for hot teas and sandwiches, but most of the adults still couldn't bring themselves to eat. It had been four and half days since the war began.

It was there that I said goodbye to Deniss; his parents had driven more than seven hundred kilometres from Latvia to pick him up at the Polish border. It made me feel as though I was losing half of myself. If you live as we did for five days, you are bound together forever. He is, and always will be, my brother. When Deniss's parents realized our group of seventeen had almost no money, they handed me two hundred euros, which I changed into Polish *zlotys* and divided evenly among us. It was like that in Poland; people were giving everything they had to anybody and everybody who needed it.

From Warsaw I flew to Toronto, and then to Montreal, where my father and brother picked me up at the airport and took me home. I walked into my mother's arms, into Somaly's, kissed my son, and then lay down on the bed next to my sleeping daughter and cried as quietly as I could.

∞

EVERY MOMENT OF THOSE DAYS OF WAR will stay with me for a long time. Even though I'm safe in Montreal, I can still feel it. I still hear the sounds of explosions and of people crying, and sometimes I dream I am feeling the shift of the train sliding across the tracks in the night. I now understand what my parents lived through in Israel when missiles rained on them from Iraq for thirty-seven days. Before the war in Ukraine, I believed I was unstoppable in many ways, immortal, but that feeling is forever gone. War takes that from you, your certainty, your belief that everything will somehow work out, the belief that you are young and untouchable. War leaves you with the ache of your own fragility. But because of my family and my children, I am strong in body and mind, and in time, I know my memories of the violence I witnessed and experienced will fade. But for those who weren't foreign citizens, all those who weren't fortunate enough to be able to leave Ukraine

Eliezer and Deniss hold the train tickets that saved their lives.
COURTESY OF THE SHERBATOV FAMILY

like me, their pain will continue for years to come. I will always be struck by the contrast between the generosity of the people in bordering nations who opened their homes to refugees in the hundreds of thousands, and of Putin's cold-blooded brutality just a few miles away. As long as this war rages, and until my last days, I will never forget the courage of the Ukrainian people or the kindness of strangers. Without them, I wouldn't be here to tell this story.

Chapter 12

What It's All For

IF THERE'S ONE THING I KNOW TO BE TRUE in my hockey life, it's that nothing ever stays the same for long. The years, the contracts and the cities always change, and my life with them.

There was only one constant in my career, no matter where I went. Every new team I ever joined had questions about my leg: how it happened, how it feels, how I relearned to skate. In Ukraine I faced a lot of the usual stares; the team trained at a pool before our first practice on the rink, and my limp is especially noticeable when I'm barefoot. I know one of the reasons I loved hockey so much as a teenager was because no one could see my disability on the ice. It simply disappeared. My left skate was my brace, it was my friend, my shield against the world. In some ways, it set me free. Just lacing it in the dressing room gave me strength before every game.

It wasn't until age twenty-four, after almost a decade of dragging my foot off the ice, that I finally decided I would wear my brace whenever I put on a pair of shoes. I was simply tired of trying to live without it. I had also accepted my disability by then and was proud of how far I had come. Even so, a small part of me continues to hope; I still attach electrodes to my leg every day to try and stimulate a bit of feeling. I suppose I refuse to give up entirely even if the doctors have. In Poland, I consulted with a neurologist to see if there was any chance of regaining even slight feeling with new medical technology. She determined it was impossible; the nerve was still completely dead. So the brace will stay with me forever, and I can live with that. If people ask me about it then I'll be proud to tell them.

When as a teenager I realized I wouldn't be drafted by the NHL, instead of ruining me, I became utterly driven to prove myself overseas. Playing hockey in Europe and Asia actually helped me overcome doubts about my own skills. It taught me to celebrate the talents I did have, and to eventually accept that I might never wear the Canadiens' jersey. When I look back at the past decade, I see achievements. Some pain, yes, but mostly success. Success overcoming a terrible injury as a child that perhaps would have been the end for other players. Success in Kazakhstan, where I raised the Cup and became a top goal scorer. And I see success with the Israeli national team, winning gold in Division II of the World Hockey Championships in 2019. Mostly I see a boy who loved hockey and who was willing to do anything to play. I'm still that boy, and always will be.

I have no idea where I'll be living in the next few years, but you can be sure I'll be on a rink somewhere, scoring

Eliezer's 2021 skates, left behind in Ukraine
DESIGNED BY GUBY CUSTOMS IN MONTREAL
REPRINTED WITH PERMISSION

goals and celebrating like I always do with a slide across the ice. I'm proud to have represented so many nations and to have brought a little joy to their fans. Every single one of those countries has made me who I am. Canada gave my family security, opportunities, and it gave me hockey. Though Canada will always be home, Israel still holds the deepest part of my heart. Immigrating to Israel saved my father's life more than thirty years ago, and during the war in Ukraine, history repeated itself when Israeli volunteers helped me and so many others to safety. I will always be grateful to everyone who played a part in that journey: to Deniss, who gave me the strength to flee with him, to the train conductors who drove us through the night, and to the volunteers who worked at the border to feed and process millions of refugees. Their compassion still overwhelms me.

I hope to give back to Israel one day, maybe the only way I know how: I'd like to finish my professional career in Tel Aviv and bring young hockey players to the game, both Arab and Jewish. I imagine a world where teenagers can meet on a rink rather than a battlefield, and where conflict will cease to exist. Borders will become meaningless and boys and girls will think of nothing but putting a puck in a net. I'm hopeful this is the world my children will inherit. Hockey can bring people together, even in the desert.

I will skate professionally for as long as I can. And when I can't anymore, I'll be at the rink to coach with my family in Montreal and to support children who understand the joy of putting on a pair of skates. I'll be on the lookout for any child who needs confidence or who may need hockey to get through a difficult time in their lives. And I'll make every possible effort to encourage children with challenges, both mental and physical, to join me on the ice. Hockey is for everyone.

I should know.